MEALS FROM THE MITTEN

MEALS FROM THE MITTEN

CELEBRATING the SEASONS in MICHIGAN

GINA FERWERDA

STORY FARM

WINTER PARK • MIAMI
SANTA BARBARA

Text copyright © 2018 by Gina Ferwerda.
Photography copyright © 2018 by Gina Ferwerda.
All rights reserved. No part of this book may be used or reproduced in any manner whatsoever without the written permission of Gina Ferwerda and Story Farm, Inc., except in the context of reviews.

Published in the United States by Story Farm, Inc.
www.story-farm.com

Library of Congress Cataloging-in-Publication Data available upon request
ISBN 978-0-9969441-7-5

EDITORIAL DIRECTOR Ashley Fraxedas
ART DIRECTOR Jason Farmand
COPY EDITOR Billie Jo Spencer, Karen Cakebread
INDEXING Amy Hall
PRODUCTION MANAGER Tina Dahl

10 9 8 7 6 5 4 3 2 1
First Edition

Printed in the United States of America

———

ALL PHOTOGRAPHY BY GINA FERWERDA EXCEPT

Todd & Brad Reed Photography
www.ToddandBradReed.com
pages 20-21, 40-41, 90-91, 118-119, 144-145

Slow Juke Photography
front cover, pages 6-7, 9, 125, 199, 208 and back cover (top left image)

Christine K. Photography
page 14 (bottom image)

For my mother-in-law, Edie. Your encouragement—or, rather, nagging—is one of the biggest reasons I wrote this book. Thank you for being my biggest cheerleader, for your guidance and for your constructive criticism, even when unsolicited. We love you and miss you every day.

CONTENTS

INTRODUCTION 8

APPY TAILS 20
SPRING 40
BURGERS & SAMMIES 64
SUMMER 90
TRAILGATING 118
FALL 144
WINTER 172

ACKNOWLEDGMENTS 198
INDEX 201

INTRODUCTION

This is a love story of food and of Michigan and how, for me, the two are intimately connected. If you had told me years ago that I'd be on TV showcasing my recipes and writing a cookbook, I would have laughed because I was so busy running hotels and resorts. But it's a story that needs to be told because, well, Michigan rocks.

IT'S A MICHIGAN THING

People from Michigan, myself very much included, have a lot of pride in our home state. And rightfully so! Beaches, sand dunes, wineries, snowmobiling trails, craft breweries … there aren't enough pages for me to talk about all the reasons I love Michigan, but here's my abridged version.

When people think "produce" and "agriculture," California usually comes to mind first. But I'm here to change that! We owe so much of our delicious fruits and veggies to Lake Michigan. Not only is the lake gorgeous, it also is the reason we have the perfect microclimate for our Fruit Belt. The "lake effect" slows the first frost in the fall and also keeps us cool in the spring—perfect conditions for our peaches, plums, apples, cherries … and so much more. Michigan yields more than 300 different agricultural products, making us second in the nation, behind California, when it comes to diversity. And Michigan leads the nation in the production of several crops, including asparagus,

WAVE CLUB WATER SPORTS RENTALS
SILVER LAKE SAND DUNES
waveclubwatersports.com

blueberries, tart cherries, cucumbers, Niagara grapes, squash and all kinds of dried beans, from black and red to cranberry.

Beyond its culinary attributes, Michigan is a true outdoor playground. We've even been named the "Trails State" for our more than 12,500-plus miles of hiking, biking, equestrian, snowmobiling, Jeeping, canoeing, snowshoeing and boating trails. We actually have more registered boaters than Florida, despite a much shorter boating season. My family and I live on Silver Lake at the Silver Lake Sand Dunes and are always outside. Depending on the time of year, you'll find us boating and stand-up paddleboarding with my Sweet Smell of Summer Burger (page 70) as the sun sets; snowmobiling our 6,500-plus miles of groomed snowmobile trails with my Muffler Meatballs (page 130) in the Muffpot on my snowmobile; off-roading in our Jeep on the 3,100-plus miles of off-road vehicle trails with my Spinach & Artichoke Bacon Bread Bowl (page 134) for a picnic lunch. That's what Michigan is about—getting out and exploring this beautiful state, and cooking and eating wherever you are.

So what is Michigan food? Like a growing number of regions, our food culture is all about being seasonal and eating local. But above all, Michigan food is not defined by the kitchen. Our dinner tables are wherever you happen to be and wherever you can eat with friends and family, be it on top of a snow-capped mountain while skiing, a picnic blanket overlooking Sleeping Bear Dunes National Lakeshore (pictured on the cover), at a winery looking out over beautiful fall colors (pictured on page 9) or at a local craft brewery festival.

That's what I specialize in. If I were to ever have my own cooking show, I would want it to be a food and travel show (showcasing Michigan,

of course) where the kitchen wasn't the main focus. I cook everywhere I go and use whatever is on hand.

Oh, did I mention that our wineries rival those in Napa and Sonoma? Don't believe me? Come and see them for yourself. Michigan will surprise you.

SHAKING CHERRIES AND PICKLE JUICE

It's funny thinking back to childhood. So many little details and experiences, which then seemed of such little importance, but which now are so profoundly important to my life.

I grew up near my grandparents' farm in Mears, Michigan. Everything revolved around the seasons, but not how you might normally think of them on a calendar. We knew the seasons by the produce growing on the farm and whether we were riding our dirt bikes or snowmobiles. We never called it "spring"; it was "asparagus season." That meant my grandparents would bag up some of the asparagus and it was time for me and my brothers to sell it to passing tourists from our little makeshift roadside stand. It wasn't "summer"; it was "cherry season," and it was short and intense. My grandmother and I would head to town (in her El Camino) and buy doughnut

holes and chocolate milk for the farming crew for their mid-morning break. When I saw apples growing on the trees, I knew it was almost time to go back to school. And when we had to trade in our dirt bikes for our snowmobiles, we knew winter was upon us and it was almost time for Christmas. We loved winter because we could snowmobile to our friends' farm going off-road through the orchards and fields.

Cherry season was always a favorite of mine. Michigan is the No. 1 producer of tart cherries in the country. On the farm, we had to handpick the sweet cherries, but the tart cherries were shaken off the trees with cool and innovative cherry shakers. My grandpa was known for his collection of vintage cars—sometimes my grandma didn't even know how many he owned—and his love of Cadillacs (I still remember the smell of the leather), for always wearing a red leather jacket and for his favorite spinach salads. I was "grandpa's girl." He let me get away with anything, and would even let me ride on the shaker during cherry season. As a child, that was the coolest thing ever. He would drive his vintage cars in parades. My favorite ones to ride in were his Model A pickup and his Model A roadster. I would sit in the little rumble seat and wave to everyone during the parades. So much fun! I also remember having cherry pit-spitting contests—yes, that's a thing in Michigan—with my brothers. I remember my older brother and a friend having a spitting contest into the pool and getting in so much trouble. (Side note: Apparently, the record distance for pit-spitting is 95 feet and 6.5 inches!)

Some of my best farm memories are pickling

with my grandma. I love, love, love pickles. My grandpa would bring in the pickling cucumbers in huge gallon-size buckets. Then, my grandma and I would start the pickling process. I was known for sneaking into the cellar where we kept all the jars and drinking all the salty, yummy juice out of the jars, leaving the cucumbers to shrivel up and dry out. One year, after one too many times of finding empty jars, my grandma got fed up and put a lock on the cellar! I guess I should thank her for keeping my blood pressure in check.

My mom always had a hot dinner on the table for the entire family at 5:30 p.m., and, on my other side of the family, I loved to be in the kitchen with my dad's sister, my Aunt Mort. She won so many baking awards, and still makes the best pies in the world. I was surrounded by so much cooking inspiration my entire childhood. Other than baking chocolate chip cookies for neighbors in high school, I really didn't start cooking on my own until I got married and had my own family. But having absorbed all that time spent on the farm and in the kitchen, it all kind of just came together for me cooking as an adult. I realize how important it is to cook around children. Maybe they aren't actively listening or participating, but they are making memories and taking it in. One day, they will remember and be able to apply those memories. For me, all those memories culminated in a career that I love … and love sharing with others.

3, 2, 1: LIVE ON TV!

I never thought I'd start a blog. In fact, I still don't consider myself a blogger. I'm just a lover of all things food and Michigan. And high heels and makeup. I show love by bringing people food (I'm not much of a hugger), so for my friend's surprise 40th birthday party, I made my favorite Caprese Burgers (page 83). I grilled all the burgers and set up a cute little burger bar with everything labeled. The party was at my friend Denise's house, who just happens to be a producer for a lifestyle show in Grand Rapids. The burgers were a huge hit at the party! Denise heard everyone raving about them and invited me to do a Fourth of July grilling segment on her show. I was so excited, but I had to create a website or blog so people watching the segment could get the recipe. Plus, it was nice to have my recipes in one place so I could send friends and family to my website instead of individually emailing recipes when they asked me for them! So I came up with the idea to do 90 burgers in 90 days on a blog to set myself apart. I called it "Boating, Boarding and Burgers," because, for me and my family, grilling burgers after the end of a long day on Silver Lake is just the best. The blog, and my TV appearances, took off from there. Now my blog is called Nom News. "Nom" meaning food and "news" representing food from my culinary travels from the North, East, West and South. In addition to showcasing local Michigan food and produce, I like to post a recipe and include different variations. I have so many people write me and ask how to make a recipe vegan, dairy-free, low-calorie or Paleo. So I try to incorporate those different variations when I create my recipes. My daughter used to be vegan, but thankfully for this meat-loving mom, she's not anymore.

I love the adrenaline rush of being on TV. When they start the countdown to going on live, "3, 2, 1," and then point, it's just this magical feeling that I can't describe. I truly enjoy showing others my recipes, tips and tricks for cooking and grilling. Some bloggers love being behind the scenes, learning all the search engine optimization algorithms to get them the most traffic. Not me. I thrive on being out there in front of it all, which, now that I think about it, also speaks to my passion of acting in plays, musicals and even movies. I feel so fortunate to put my love of entertaining and cooking together into a new career that is so rewarding.

One of my favorite TV segments was for National Chocolate Cake Day on *Good Morning America*. GMA flew me to New York City to compete for who could make the best chocolate cake. The segment was hosted by GMA anchors Jesse Palmer, Amy Robach and Lara Spencer. The judges were the New York/New Jersey Bakers Club and celebrity chef Rocco DiSpirito. My Pretzel Crusted Chocolate Cake with Peanut Butter Frosting (page 94) came in first place! I was so happy to win, but mostly, this proud Michigander was happy to bring some food notoriety to her home state.

MEALS ARE MEMORIES

My favorite saying is, "Recipes are simple ingredients and directions. It's not until you make a memory that they truly become meals." Recipes are one of the best ways to preserve your family history and memories.

A few years ago, I realized that I still had a lot of family recipes that I needed to gather before, well, it was too late. So, I called my mother-in-law, Edie, and my aunts, and asked if I could borrow their treasured recipes and make copies of them. Everyone was very happy to oblige, although Edie said I only had one week with her collection. So, I made copies of everything and even had them pass along memories that went with each recipe.

Edie passed away a few years later, making those copies of her handwritten recipe collection—a collection she had accumulated for 80 years—extraordinarily precious.

After that experience, I decided to start a social media campaign that I called, "Meals are Memories." I created a 5-minute YouTube video that I posted around Thanksgiving, because I realized the six weeks between Thanksgiving and New Years is the most time you'll spend cooking around family and friends the entire year. In the video, I implored people to start collecting treasured family recipes, and shared my experience with collecting my own family recipes. I was shocked by the positive feedback I received. I even had a friend who was able to save a family favorite cheesecake recipe that they thought was lost after their aunt developed Alzheimer's disease.

There are two things that I'd like you to take away from this book. First, I hope it inspires you to compile your family's special recipes to help preserve your family history. While you're at it, write down notes and memories to go with each recipe. Future generations will thank you! And the second is that I hope this book inspires you to have a love and appreciation for Michigan and Michigan food.

So, here is a piece of my family heritage—my favorite Michigan-inspired recipes. *Welcome to Meals from the Mitten*!

—Gina

LAKE MICHIGAN SUNSET

1

APPY TAILS
FOR ALL SEASONS

I love appetizers and party food, which is why this is one of my favorite chapters in this book. (I can't really pick a favorite; that would be like picking a favorite child!) What is an "appy tail"? Well, it's a combination of an amazing appetizer and a signature cocktail or mocktail. I wish more restaurants would offer this! All too often, I get to a restaurant and am so hungry that I need to have a quick bite. I always end up ordering a Bloody Mary just so I can have the pickled veggie skewer. But I'd much rather be able to order one of my Silver Sunset Cocktails (page 38).

These appetizers and cocktails combine the best that Michigan has to offer—one happy sip and bite at a time.

Mimosas, of course, are great for brunches and early morning weekends on the lake. But add in Michigan black sweet cherries and decadent brownies, and now it's really a party. These are always on my menu when I host a bridal or baby shower. A refreshing twist on a great classic that's so easy to make.

SERVES 4

BLACK CHERRY MIMOSAS
WITH TRIPLE CHERRY BROWNIE BITE SKEWERS

MAKE MIMOSAS

Roughly chop cherries and add to a small bowl, then mix in almond extract. Equally divide cherry mixture among the bottoms of 4 champagne flutes. Add 1 ounce of orange juice to each flute and top with sparkling wine, prosecco or champagne.

MAKE SKEWERS

Add a cherry to each skewer, followed by a cubed brownie bite and then another cherry. Serve with Black Cherry Mimosas.

BLACK CHERRY MIMOSAS

SERVES 4

- 8 black sweet cherries, stemmed and pitted
- ⅛ teaspoon almond extract
- 4 ounces orange juice
- Sparkling wine, prosecco or champagne

GARNISH

Triple Cherry Brownie Bite Skewers (see recipe below)

TRIPLE CHERRY BROWNIE BITE SKEWERS

SERVES 4

- 8 black sweet cherries, pitted
- 4 cocktail skewers (at least 3 inches long)
- 1 Triple Cherry Brownie (page 117), cut into bite-size pieces

NOTE

I love to use Chateau Chantal Tonight sparkling wine for this recipe.

APPY TAILS

APPLE CIDER MOSCOW MULE

SERVES 1

- 2 ounces apple cider
- 2 ounces vodka
- 2 ounces ginger beer or Vernors ginger ale
- ½ ounce freshly squeezed lime juice

GARNISH

- Cinnamon stick
- Lime wedge

CARAMEL APPLE CHEESECAKE SKEWERS

SERVES 4

- 1 Michigan apple, cored and sliced
- 8 pieces Ritzy Rich Bars (page 196), cut into bite-size pieces
- 4 cocktail skewers (at least 6 inches long)

GARNISH

- Caramel
- Sea salt

NOTE

For a mocktail version, replace vodka with ginger ale or lemon-lime soda.

Apples are the largest and most valuable fruit crop that we have in Michigan. I grew up with an apple cider mill about a block away. When I think of apple cider, I instantly think of fall colors, cool weather and caramel apples. These caramel cheesecake bites and apples are a perfect pair for this Moscow Mule. Since we are known for our ginger ale in Michigan, substitute it for the ginger beer for a less gingery flavor and an extra kick of carbonation. The caramel cheesecakes bites in this recipe are from my Ritzy Rich Bars (page 196), but instead of adding chocolate and pecans for a turtle bar, I add sea salt to the caramel and pair it with cubes of your favorite Michigan apple.

SERVES 4

APPLE CIDER MOSCOW MULES
WITH CARAMEL APPLE CHEESECAKE SKEWERS

MAKE MOSCOW MULE

Pour apple cider, vodka, ginger beer or ginger ale and lime juice into a copper cup. Stir well and fill rest of cup with crushed ice. Serve with a cinnamon stick and a lime wedge.

MAKE CHEESECAKE SKEWERS

Evenly divide apple slices and cheesecake pieces onto skewers. Drizzle caramel over skewers and sprinkle with sea salt.

ASSEMBLE

Make 4 Apple Cider Moscow Mules, and top each with a Caramel Apple Cheesecake Skewer.

Blackberries are abundant every summer in Michigan. They are so juicy and delicious, and are a perfect addition to a refreshingly minty mojito. The salami, mint and mozzarella skewer offers the perfect bite in between each sip.

SERVES 4

BLACKBERRY MOJITOS
WITH SALAMI, MINT & MOZZARELLA SKEWERS

MAKE MOJITO

Gently muddle blackberries, mint leaves, sugar and lime juice. Add rum and top with soda water or lemon-lime soda. Serve on the rocks with fresh mint leaves, blackberries and a lime wedge.

MAKE SKEWERS

Fold salami slices in half, and then in half again. Add 1 mint leaf to a skewer, followed by a folded slice of salami, a mozzarella ball and a blackberry. Repeat with remaining skewers.

ASSEMBLE

Make 4 Blackberry Mojitos, and serve each with a Salami, Mint & Mozzarella Skewer.

BLACKBERRY MOJITO
SERVES 1

- ¼ cup fresh blackberries, plus extra for garnish
- 6 mint leaves
- 2 teaspoons sugar
- 1 ounce freshly squeezed lime juice
- 2 ounces light rum
- Soda water or lemon-lime soda

GARNISH

Lime wedge

SALAMI, MINT & MOZZARELLA SKEWERS
SERVES 4

- 4 salami slices
- 4 fresh mint leaves
- 4 fresh mozzarella balls
- 4 fresh large blackberries
- 4 cocktail skewers (at least 4 inches long)

NOTE

For a mocktail version, replace rum with lemon-lime soda.

I love Bloody Marys, and I also love dirty martinis. So, naturally, I combined the two of them. Confession—I drink my Bloody Marys without alcohol. I know, it's crazy! But I love spicy Bloody Mary mix so much that I actually think the alcohol ruins the drink. But, on the other side of the spectrum, I drink my martinis fully loaded and extra dry with blue cheese-stuffed olives. In fact, I love the olives so much that I was inspired to come up with this drink. I'd always eat all of the olives before even tasting my drink, so I decided to line the inside rim of the glass with blue cheese (not the outside, because it sticks to my lipstick). This way, you get that bold, pungent cheese flavor with every sip. You can never have too much of a good thing.

SERVES 1

BLUE CHEESE RIMMED
BLOODY MARY-TINI

- 1 tablespoon blue cheese crumbles
- Splash of milk or cream
- 2 ounces vodka
- 1 ounce dry vermouth
- 3 ounces Bloody Mary mix
- ½ ounce dill pickle juice (substitute: olive juice)
- ¼ teaspoon horseradish
- ⅛ teaspoon celery salt
- 1 cocktail skewer (at least 7 inches long)

OPTIONAL GARNISHES

- Celery
- Pickled asparagus
- Dill pickles
- Blue cheese olives
- Cocktail onions
- Candied bacon
- Shrimp
- Pickled garlic scapes
- Pepperoncini

In a small bowl, combine blue cheese crumbles and a splash of milk or cream, then add a thin layer of the blue cheese mixture to the inside rim of a martini glass. Set aside until ready to use.

Add 2 ice cubes to a martini shaker. Next add vodka, vermouth, Bloody Mary mix, pickle juice, horseradish and celery salt. Shake well. Pour the Bloody Mary mixture into the glass. Skewer optional garnishes and add to the glass.

COCONUT SHRIMP SKEWERS

SERVES 4+

Canola oil or any high-smoke-point oil, for frying

½ cup coconut flour

1 teaspoon House Seasoning (page 96)

3 eggs, beaten

1 cup panko breadcrumbs

1 cup shredded sweetened coconut

1 pound colossal shrimp with tails attached, peeled and deveined

Cocktail skewers (at least 4 inches in length)

¼ cup pickled ginger

2 large grapefruits or oranges, sliced and halved

Sweet & Sour Pickled Ginger Sauce (recipe below)

SWEET & SOUR PICKLED GINGER SAUCE

½ cup pineapple juice

1½ tablespoons rice wine vinegar

1 tablespoon sugar

1 teaspoon cornstarch

3 teaspoons soy sauce

1 teaspoon ketchup

¼ teaspoon red-pepper flakes

1 tablespoon chopped pickled ginger

NOTE

This recipe will make more than 4 skewers. Serve the extra skewers on a platter alongside the cocktails.

My home in Silver Lake is surrounded by breathtaking sand dunes. They're truly awe-inspiring. There are more than 2,000 acres of dunes in Silver Lake State Park, and they're the only dunes east of Utah that you can drive on. We're a Jeep family, and we love cruising and climbing the dunes. After a long day of dune docking, this cocktail is the one to make. The grapefruit juice is so refreshing, and the coconut shrimp skewers are so crunchy and delicious with the sweet and sour sauce. My secret to breading is coconut flour.

SERVES 4

DUNE DOCKER COCKTAILS
WITH COCONUT SHRIMP SKEWERS

MAKE SKEWERS

In a deep, heavy pot, heat 2 to 3 inches of oil over medium-high heat until oil reaches 350°F.

Set up a dredging station with 3 mixing bowls. Add flour and House Seasoning to one bowl, add eggs to the second bowl, and add panko and shredded coconut to the third bowl. Make sure every bowl is thoroughly mixed. Dredge shrimp in flour, then in eggs and finally in panko-coconut mixture.

Fry shrimp to golden brown, about 1 to 2 minutes per side if using raw shrimp. Fry 1 to 2 minutes total if using cooked shrimp. *(Note: Do not overcook shrimp or they will turn rubbery.)*

Add 1 fried coconut shrimp to a skewer, followed by some pickled ginger and a piece of fruit. Drizzle on some Sweet & Sour Pickled Ginger Sauce. Repeat process with remaining shrimp, ginger and fruit.

MAKE GINGER SAUCE

In a saucepan over medium heat, add all ingredients and whisk together. Bring to a simmer, then turn off heat and let cool. Serve drizzled over Coconut Shrimp Skewers.

MAKE COCKTAIL

Rim a tall glass with a lime wedge, then coat with coarse salt. Fill glass halfway with ice. Add tequila, triple sec, grapefruit juice and pickled ginger juice. Squeeze 2 lime wedges into glass, then stir. Top with sparkling water.

ASSEMBLE

Make 4 Dune Docker Cocktails, and serve each with a Coconut Shrimp Skewer.

DUNE DOCKER COCKTAIL

SERVES 1

1 lime, cut into wedges

Coarse salt

2 ounces blanco tequila

1½ ounces triple sec

3 ounces grapefruit juice

¼ ounce pickled ginger juice

Grapefruit or lime flavored sparkling water

These shakes remind me of Christmas Eve at my grandparents', when, for just that one night, they would dust off the Galliano and make Golden Cadillacs. Of course, when I was a kid, we got the mocktail version. This vanilla-anise flavored cocktail is considered a digestif, or an after-dinner drink, which is why I turned it into an after-dinner dessert cocktail. Golden Cadillacs originated from California but somehow became a Michigan drink, probably because Michigan claims anything car-related … and rightfully so.

SERVES 4

GOLDEN CADILLAC SHAKES
WITH CHOCOLATE GANACHE & GRAHAM CRACKER-TOFFEE S'MORE SKEWERS

MAKE CADILLAC SHAKES

Blend together Galliano, white crème de cocoa and ice cream. Drizzle chocolate syrup over the inside of 4 glasses, then pour equal amounts of the ice cream mixture into each glass.

> NOTE: For a mocktail version, replace Galliano and white crème de cocoa with ¼ cup of malted milk powder and ⅓ cup milk.

MAKE TOFFEE S'MORE SKEWERS

Place graham crackers and toffee pieces in a food processor and finely grind.

Add chocolate to a medium-size bowl. In a small saucepan, bring cream to a slow boil, then pour over chocolate and let sit for 5 minutes. Whisk together chocolate and cream to make chocolate ganache.

Thread 1 marshmallow onto each skewer. Dip marshmallow into the chocolate ganache and sprinkle with some graham cracker-and-toffee mixture. Let cool. Repeat process for remaining skewers. Serve with Golden Cadillac Shakes.

GOLDEN CADILLAC SHAKES
SERVES 4

2 ounces Galliano
2 ounces white crème de cocoa
1 pint vanilla ice cream

GARNISH

Chocolate syrup

CHOCOLATE GANACHE & GRAHAM CRACKER-TOFFEE S'MORE SKEWERS
SERVES 4

2 graham crackers
2 tablespoons toffee pieces

CHOCOLATE GANACHE

4 ounces semi-sweet chocolate chips
¼ cup heavy cream

4 regular-size marshmallows
4 cocktail skewers (at least 3 inches in length)

NOTE

Refrigerate any leftover ganache. The cold ganache makes delicious truffles: Simply roll a small amount of ganache into a ball, then roll in the crushed graham crackers and toffee mixture.

The tart cherry juice and blood orange bitters give this Manhattan its Michigan touch. If you're a Manhattan fan, this will be your new go-to. I mean, it has candied bacon and bourbon-soaked black cherries. What could be better?!

SERVES 4

MICHIGAN MANHATTAN COCKTAILS
WITH ANCHO CHILI CANDIED BACON & BOURBON-SOAKED BLACK CHERRIES SKEWERS

MICHIGAN MANHATTAN
SERVES 1

- 2 ounces rye whiskey
- ¾ ounce sweet vermouth
- 3 dashes blood orange bitters
- ¼ ounce Montmorency tart cherry juice

ANCHO CHILI CANDIED BACON

- 4 slices thick-cut bacon
- 1 tablespoon brown sugar
- ¼ teaspoon ancho chili powder

BOURBON-SOAKED BLACK CHERRIES

- ½ cup sweet black cherries, pitted
- ⅛ teaspoon almond extract
- 2 ounces New Holland beer barrel bourbon
- 4 cocktail skewers (at least 4 inches long)

MAKE MANHATTAN

Pour whiskey, vermouth, bitters and cherry juice into a tall glass with cracked ice and stir. Strain into a chilled cocktail glass and serve straight up.

MAKE CANDIED BACON

Preheat oven to 375°F.

Place bacon on a slotted pan or parchment paper-lined pan and evenly coat with brown sugar. Sprinkle with chili powder and bake for 15 to 18 minutes, or until thoroughly cooked.

MAKE BLACK CHERRIES

Soak black cherries in almond extract and bourbon for at least 2 hours, or overnight (preferred).

ASSEMBLE

Thread candied bacon and black cherries onto 4 skewers. Make 4 Michigan Manhattan cocktails, and serve each with an Ancho Chili Candied Bacon & Bourbon-Soaked Black Cherries Skewer.

I like to make things easy and effortless when I'm entertaining, and these Peach Bellinis are a great way to do just that. My family loves the peach version, but feel free to substitute any fruit that you like. Make this ahead of time and freeze the fruit puree, then just slightly thaw it when you are ready to entertain. A Bellini bar is a great thing to set up for bridal showers.

SERVES 4

PEACH BELLINIS
WITH MOZZARELLA, BASIL & PROSCIUTTO PEACH SKEWERS

MAKE BELLINIS

Place peaches, sugar, lemon juice, simple syrup and triple sec in a blender or food processor, and blend or process until all ingredients are well-incorporated.

Add 2 ounces of peach puree to each of 4 champagne flutes, then top with sparkling wine, prosecco or champagne.

MAKE PEACH SKEWERS

Add 1 quartered peach to a skewer followed by a mozzarella ball. Add a fresh basil leaf and a prosciutto or prosciutto-wrapped mozzarella slice. Repeat with remaining skewers. Serve with Peach Bellinis.

PEACH BELLINIS

SERVES 4

- 1 (16-ounce) bag frozen peaches, thawed
- 2 tablespoons sugar
- Juice of 1 lemon
- ⅓ cup simple syrup (equal parts water and sugar)
- ⅓ cup triple sec
- Sparkling wine, prosecco or champagne

MOZZARELLA, BASIL & PROSCIUTTO PEACH SKEWERS

SERVES 4

- 1 fresh peach, seeded and quartered
- 4 fresh mozzarella balls
- 4 fresh basil leaves
- 4 slices prosciutto or prosciutto-wrapped mozzarella slices
- 4 cocktail skewers (at least 3 inches long)

NOTE

Leftover peach puree can be frozen for up to 3 months.

Frozen peach puree equals 1¾ cups. Add ⅓ cup simple syrup and ⅓ cup triple sec to the puree, and that equals approximately 2½ cups.

If using fresh peaches for the puree: Blend 2 fresh peaches, peeled and seeded, along with 1 tablespoon of sugar and 1 tablespoon of lemon juice, and that equals approximately ¾ cup.

APPY TAILS

JALAPEÑO PINEAPPLE FILET MIGNON KABOBS

SERVES 6

MARINADE

- ⅓ cup BLiS Michigan Maple Soy sauce
- ⅓ cup pineapple orange juice
- 1 tablespoon sherry vinegar
- 1 tablespoon red wine vinegar
- 1 clove garlic, minced
- 1 tablespoon minced jalapeño

- 1 pound filet mignon steaks (approximately 2 to 3 steaks, each 2 inches thick), cut into 1-inch cubes
- 1 small red onion, cut into bite-size pieces
- 2 bell peppers, cut into bite-size pieces
- 2 cups pineapple chunks, cut into bite-size pieces
- 6 skewers (at least 7 inches long)

JALAPEÑO PINEAPPLE MARGARITA

SERVES 1

- 3 ounces pineapple juice
- 2 ounces tequila
- Juice of ½ lime
- ½ ounce pickled jalapeño juice

GARNISH

- Jalapeño slices
- Fresh cilantro leaves

NOTE

If using wooden skewers, soak in water for at least 30 minutes prior to grilling to prevent wood from burning.

I may be a tad biased, but Michigan has the most beautiful sunsets in the world. They're so beautiful that crowds erupt in applause on Lake Michigan's beaches as the sun sets. In fact, the only thing that can make a sunset better is enjoying this spicy margarita and filet mignon kabobs with friends and family. This cocktail is a summer sunset and a night of grilling in a glass.

SERVES 6

SILVER SUNSET COCKTAILS
JALAPEÑO PINEAPPLE MARGARITAS & FILET MIGNON KABOBS

MAKE FILET MIGNON KABOBS

Preheat oven to 425°F. Line a baking sheet with aluminum foil.

Preheat grill to medium-high heat.

In a medium-size bowl, mix together all marinade ingredients. Reserve 2 tablespoons of marinade for roasting vegetables; set aside. Place meat into a bowl, cover and marinate for at least 30 minutes.

Place onion, peppers and pineapple on baking sheet, then pour reserved marinade over top. Roast for 10 minutes.

Thread roasted veggies, fruit and meat onto skewers, then grill for 5 to 7 minutes for medium-rare doneness. Turn skewers every 1 to 2 minutes to grill all sides evenly. Remove skewers from grill.

MAKE MARGARITAS

Add pineapple juice, tequila, lime juice and jalapeño juice to a cocktail shaker, along with some ice. Cover, shake and strain into a chilled martini glass. Garnish with jalapeño slices and cilantro.

ASSEMBLE

Make 6 Jalapeño Pineapple Margaritas, and serve each with a Filet Mignon Kabob.

2

SPRING

After a fun-filled (but sometimes long) Michigan winter, everyone is waiting for spring weather—and spring produce. Especially me! I grew up with a farming family. My grandparents and uncle grew everything from asparagus to cherries to apples. Michigan is one of the leading producers of asparagus in the nation.

You know it's spring when you start seeing fresh rhubarb. Because of the Lake Effect we experience here, we have an unbelievable Fruit Belt near the shores of Lake Michigan, and I love to take full, delicious advantage with my Strawberry Feta Spinach Salad (page 58) and Rhubarb & Strawberry Pretzel Crumble (page 62). And you can't think of spring in Michigan without hunting for those elusive morel mushrooms. We have been hunting and cooking them for as long as I can remember. Morels are one of springtime's finest delicacies and worth the trouble finding, especially for Spring Morel Risotto (page 61).

Beyond produce, springtime means the opening of the Detroit Tigers baseball season and, since my husband is Dutch, we look forward to all the beautiful tulips on display at the Tulip Time festival in Holland, Michigan. At this time of year, we are also getting ready to open our seasonal resorts for the summer. The lakes freeze over every winter, so we trade our snow skis and snowmobiles for boats and Jeeps, and finally put our docks back in as spring melts the ice.

CHERRY ORCHARD IN WEST MICHIGAN

Asparagus is the first spring crop that pops up in Michigan, and you could say we're a little obsessed with it—we even have a National Asparagus Festival and crown an Asparagus Queen where I live in Oceana County. I've been working with the Asparagus Advisory Board for years to come up with creative, delicious asparagus recipes, and this guacamole is one of my favorites. The whole recipe uses only one avocado to a pound of asparagus, so you lose a lot of the fat but retain the creamy, velvety consistency. Purists rest assured—I guarantee you won't notice the difference. I serve this guacamole all spring and summer long on tacos or with Michigan La Fiesta chips.

SERVES 4

ANCHO CHILE ASPARAGUS GUACAMOLE

- 1 pound Michigan asparagus, chopped and steamed
- 1 avocado, halved, seeded and peeled
- 1 clove garlic
- 3 tablespoons green pepper Tabasco sauce (or 1 tablespoon fresh, chopped jalapeño)
- ¼ cup cilantro leaves
- ¼ teaspoon ancho chile powder
- 1 teaspoon celery salt
- ½ teaspoon black pepper
- 1 teaspoon cumin
- Juice of 1 lime
- 2 tablespoons red onion, minced
- ½ cup plum tomatoes, quartered

Add all of the ingredients, except for the onions and tomatoes, to a food processor and pulse until thoroughly combined. Transfer to a bowl, then gently fold in the onion and tomatoes. Serve with tortilla chips or on tacos.

NOTE

To store fresh asparagus, stand asparagus straight up in jar with at least 1 inch of water. Loosely cover spears with a breathable bag (I use paper). Change water out every couple days.

Michigan is the only state to hand-pick our asparagus. It's picked close to the ground, snapping it off at the base. Although labor intensive, this method produces a more tender spear.

People from Michigan and the Midwest love to throw huge graduation parties. There are at least three things you can expect at these graduation parties: hundreds of guests, asparagus roll-ups and deep-fried asparagus. I decided to combine two of these party staples to create a really decadent treat because you can't go wrong with anything that's fried and has cream cheese.

SERVES 12

DEEP-FRIED ASPARAGUS ROLL-UPS
WITH CHIPOTLE LIME DIPPING SAUCE

ASPARAGUS ROLL-UPS

12 fresh Michigan asparagus spears

4 ounces plain cream cheese, softened

12 slices deli ham, thinly sliced

BATTER

1 cup flour

1 teaspoon salt

2 eggs

½ cup milk

½ teaspoon granulated garlic

½ teaspoon dill weed

2 cups panko breadcrumbs

Oil, for deep-frying

CHIPOTLE LIME DIPPING SAUCE

½ cup sour cream

1½ tablespoons adobo sauce

1 teaspoon lime juice

1 teaspoon dill weed

1 tablespoon minced chives

Add all ingredients to a small, non-reactive bowl. Mix well, cover and refrigerate until ready to use.

NOTE

Substitute plain cream cheese with flavored cream cheese, such as garden vegetable, chive and onion, jalapeño or chipotle.

Make sure to use a high-smoke-point oil, such as canola, vegetable, avocado or peanut.

MAKE ASPARAGUS ROLL-UPS

Trim asparagus spears to the same length as the ham slices.

Blanch asparagus for 1 to 2 minutes. (Or you can place the spears on a microwaveable plate covered with a damp paper towel and heat on high for 2 minutes.) Remember: the thinner the spear, the less cooking time needed.

Add a thin layer of cream cheese to each ham slice. Place an asparagus spear at one end of ham slice and roll up. Do this for the remaining spears, then refrigerate until ready to dredge in the batter.

MAKE BATTER

Set up 3 dishes. In the first dish, add flour and salt. In the second dish, whisk together eggs, milk, garlic and dill. In the third dish, add the breadcrumbs.

ASSEMBLE

Dip each ham-and-cheese asparagus spear in flour, followed by egg mixture and then panko. Lay flat until ready to fry.

Add oil to a deep-fryer or a large skillet, just enough to cover spears. Heat to 365°F. Gently add asparagus spears to oil and fry for 3 to 4 minutes or until golden brown.

Serve with Chipotle Lime Dipping Sauce.

My high school friends and I would always go to the deli in our local grocery for lunch. And every day we'd buy the same thing—this chicken salad. We lived on it (and the 25-cent cookie dough sold at the cafeteria). This recipe is exactly how I remember the deli's tasting. Pick your mayonnaise preference, but I feel the tanginess of miracle whip is very important.

SERVES 6 to 8

SWISS CHICKEN PASTA SALAD

PREPARE PASTA & PEAS

Add pasta to boiling, salted water and cook according to directions on package. During the last 2 minutes of cooking, add peas to pasta water. Drain and rinse with cold water for 1 to 2 minutes.

MAKE DRESSING

In a large bowl, mix all dressing ingredients together.

ASSEMBLE

Add pasta and peas to the dressing mixture, and fold all ingredients together. Cover and refrigerate until well-chilled. Serve with or in lettuce leaves. Garnish with fresh dill, radishes or cherry tomatoes.

PASTA & PEAS

- 1 pound pasta, such as rotini or cavatappi
- 2 cups fresh Michigan peas, washed and shelled (or thawed frozen peas)

DRESSING

- 2 cups shredded or cubed cooked chicken
- 1 cup diced celery
- 2 cups salad dressing or mayonnaise
- 6 ounces cubed Swiss cheese
- 1 teaspoon salt
- 1 teaspoon freshly ground pepper
- ¾ teaspoon dill weed
- ½ teaspoon granulated garlic

Bibb or romaine lettuce leaves

OPTIONAL GARNISHES

Fresh dill

Sliced radishes

Sliced cherry tomatoes

Zest of 1 lemon

NOTE

Optional: Add the Swiss Chicken Pasta Salad from above to a casserole dish to make Swiss Chicken Pasta Casserole. Simply top pasta with 2 cups shredded cheddar cheese and 1 cup panko breadcrumbs. Bake at 350°F for 30 to 40 minutes.

Food is so trendy. Cauliflower crust got popular but my husband doesn't like smelling cruciferous vegetables (think: broccoli, bok choy, Brussels sprouts, cabbage) cooking in the house. He says it stinks for days! So, since Michigan is famous for asparagus and I love my husband, I subbed in asparagus. The result is delicious and low-carb. I guarantee you won't miss the bread.

SERVES 8

ASPARAGUS CRUST
WHITE CHICKEN PIZZA

ASPARAGUS CRUST

- 2 cups cut-up fresh or frozen Michigan asparagus, blanched
- 1 egg
- ⅔ cup grated Parmesan
- ⅔ cup shredded mozzarella
- 1 tablespoon lemon pepper seasoning

WHITE SAUCE

- 2 tablespoons butter
- ¼ cup chopped leeks
- 1 clove garlic, minced
- 1 tablespoon flour
- ¾ cup milk
- ¼ cup grated Parmesan

TOPPINGS

- 1 cup cubed rotisserie chicken
- 1 cup shredded mozzarella
- ½ cup frozen green peas, thawed
- ½ cup cut-up fresh or frozen Michigan asparagus, blanched and seasoned with some avocado oil and lemon pepper seasoning
- ¼ cup chopped prosciutto
- Fresh chives or basil, for garnish

NOTE

Lemon pepper seasoning substitute: lemon zest, salt, black pepper and granulated garlic.

Preheat oven to 375°F.

MAKE ASPARAGUS CRUST

Add blanched asparagus to a food processor and puree until smooth. In a large bowl, add asparagus puree, egg, Parmesan, mozzarella and lemon pepper seasoning. Mix all ingredients until thoroughly combined.

Press asparagus mixture into a circular shape on a parchment paper-lined pizza stone (or baking sheet). Press a layer of paper towel over the crust and gently press down to remove excess moisture. Repeat one more time, or until paper towel is no longer absorbing moisture. Discard wet paper towels.

Bake for 12 to 13 minutes.

MAKE WHITE SAUCE

Add butter, leeks and garlic to a saucepan and cook for 3 to 4 minutes over medium heat. Slowly whisk in flour and cook for 1 to 2 minutes. Slowly add in milk, continually whisking, and cook until thickened. Add Parmesan, then remove from heat and set aside.

ASSEMBLE

Pour the white sauce over the partially baked asparagus crust, and top with chicken and mozzarella. Add peas, asparagus and prosciutto. Bake for an additional 5 to 8 minutes, or until cheese is thoroughly melted. Garnish with fresh chives or basil.

Seems like I'm constantly cooking for large groups, be it our employees at Wave Club Water Sports and Wet Head Beach Shop, or for lots of friends out on the lake. You'll rarely find me making something for just my husband and me. And since it's a pain to make individual egg sandwiches, sheet pan eggs are the best way to go. You can also make them ahead and even double it (which I always do). Toss in any vegetable and cheese you find in your fridge. Just remember: the more the toppings, the longer you'll need to cook the eggs. When serving, cut out the eggs to fit any shape of bread you have on hand.

SERVES 12

ASPARAGUS & HAVARTI DILL SHEET PAN EGGS

Preheat oven to 325°F. Liberally spray a quarter-sheet baking pan with nonstick cooking spray.

Whisk together eggs, milk, salt, pepper, garlic and dill in a large bowl. Pour egg mixture into sheet pan.

Using a vegetable peeler, shave asparagus spears into thin ribbons. Evenly distribute the shaved asparagus and shredded cheese on top of the egg mixture.

Bake for 20 to 30 minutes, or until no longer runny.

Let set for 5 minutes, then cut into desired shapes and sizes. Serve hot with some fresh salsa or hot sauce. Or make this into an egg sandwich: simply cut the eggs into the same size of the bread you are using. Cut eggs into round shapes for bagels or English muffins.

12 eggs
1 cup milk
1 teaspoon salt
¼ teaspoon freshly ground pepper
½ teaspoon granulated garlic
¼ teaspoon dill weed
5 fresh Michigan asparagus spears
1 cup shredded Havarti dill cheese

NOTE

Feel free to add some cooked meats like ham, bacon or sausage. Add additional vegetables or different cheeses. These sheet pan eggs can serve as a blank canvas: simply add your family's favorite ingredients and bake.

Let the kids get involved and use cookie cutters to cut out the eggs in unique shapes and sizes.

This is a recipe every woman will get down with. Whether you're throwing a baby shower or hosting a birthday party, these Parmesan cups are just really beautiful and great for entertaining. I will tell you, the cups are a little tricky to make, but it's merely a timing issue—you have to flip the warm, soft cheese over the tin at just the right time or they won't make the right shape. But it's worth the trouble for your guests to enjoy these hand-held salads.

SERVES 6 to 8

ASPARAGUS SPRING SALAD
IN PARMESAN CHEESE CUPS

- 2 cups fresh Michigan asparagus spears, cut into bite-size pieces
- 1½ cups shredded Parmesan cheese

HONEY DIJON RED WINE VINAIGRETTE

- 1½ tablespoons Dijon mustard
- 2 tablespoons Michigan honey
- Juice of 1 Meyer lemon
- 3 tablespoons red wine vinegar
- 1 clove garlic, minced
- ¼ teaspoon salt
- ¼ teaspoon freshly ground pepper
- ¼ teaspoon Sriracha seasoning
- ½ cup sunflower oil

- 4 cups mixed salad greens
- 1 cup cherry tomatoes, quartered
- Freshly grated or shaved Parmesan cheese, for garnish

NOTE

Dressing makes approximately 1 cup. Cover and refrigerate remaining dressing.

Meyer lemon juice substitute: juice ½ a lemon and ½ an orange.

TIP

If the cheese hardens after baking but before it is formed into a cup, it can be resoftened. Place the Parmesan crisp on a microwaveable plate and heat on high for 3 seconds. Once soft, immediately drape over the back side of the mini muffin tin.

Preheat oven to 375°F.

PREPARE ASPARAGUS

Steam or blanch asparagus until tender-crisp, about 3 to 4 minutes.

MAKE CHEESE CUPS

On a silicone or parchment paper-lined baking sheet, add 2 tablespoons of Parmesan cheese in a round and gently pat down. Repeat, keeping space between each cheese round. Bake for 2 to 3 minutes, then cool for 30 seconds. Lift each round with a spatula and drape over the back side of a mini muffin tin. Set aside and let cheese form into cups.

MAKE HONEY DIJON RED WINE VINAIGRETTE

In a small bowl, whisk together Dijon, honey, lemon juice, vinegar, garlic, salt, pepper and Sriracha seasoning. Slowly add sunflower oil while vigorously whisking until dressing is emulsified.

ASSEMBLE

In a large bowl, add mixed greens, tomatoes and asparagus. Drizzle ¼ cup of dressing on greens and gently toss together. Add more dressing, if needed. Add a pinch of salad inside each Parmesan cup.

Add the remaining salad to a large platter, then top with the Parmesan crisp salad cups. Garnish with freshly grated or shaved Parmesan cheese.

Chicken satay, as delicious as it is, can be really fattening. In this recipe, I save tons of calories by using peanut butter powder instead of actual peanut butter. In just two tablespoons, it will save you about 14 grams of fat, but you lose nothing else. It's still flavorful and the consistency is spot on. This dish is great hot or cold the next day. My daughters love this.

SERVES 8

SOBA NOODLE ASPARAGUS CHICKEN SATAY

DAIRY FREE

PEANUT SAUCE

- ½ cup peanut butter powder
- ⅓ cup low-sodium soy sauce
- ⅓ cup rice wine vinegar
- 2 tablespoons brown sugar
- 1 tablespoon garlic paste
- 1 tablespoon ginger paste
- 2 teaspoons toasted sesame oil
- ¼ cup canola oil
- ½ cup water

8 boneless, skinless chicken thighs, cut in half lengthwise

NOODLES

- 12 ounces soba noodles
- 1 cup red cabbage, thinly sliced
- 1 pound fresh Michigan asparagus, cut into bite-size pieces
- ½ cup leeks, washed and thinly sliced
- 1 cup bell peppers, thinly sliced

Skewers (if using wooden skewers, soak in water for 30 minutes prior to grilling)

OPTIONAL GARNISHES

- Sriracha
- Red-pepper flakes
- Mandarin oranges
- Cilantro
- Blue cheese crumbles

MAKE PEANUT SAUCE

In a saucepan over medium-high heat, whisk together peanut butter powder, soy sauce, vinegar, brown sugar, garlic paste, ginger paste, oils and water. Bring to a simmer, then reduce heat to medium-low, and cook for 5 minutes or until slightly thickened. Let cool and set aside.

MARINATE CHICKEN

Add chicken and ¼ cup of peanut sauce to a large, resealable bag. Seal and refrigerate for 30 minutes, or up to 2 hours.

PREPARE NOODLES

Add noodles, cabbage, asparagus, leeks and peppers to a large pot of boiling water. Bring back to a boil, then reduce heat to medium-low and cook for 3 minutes. Reserve ½ cup of water, then drain and set aside.

ASSEMBLE

Remove chicken from bag and discard marinade. Thread chicken onto skewers and grill over medium-high heat for 3 to 4 minutes each side, or until done. Add the remaining peanut sauce to the noodle mixture. Lightly toss together over medium heat until warm. Add some reserved water to thin the sauce, if needed.

To serve, equally divide noodle mixture among 8 plates and top each with 2 chicken skewers.

TIP

GLUTEN-FREE: Use coconut aminos instead of soy sauce, and make sure soba noodles are 100 percent buckwheat with no wheat fillers.

VEGAN: Use tofu or mushrooms instead of chicken, coconut aminos instead of soy sauce and coconut sugar instead of brown sugar.

By the end of winter, I'm so tired of the cold and so ready for warmer weather. These pineapple bowls are delicious reminders that summer is right around the corner! The presentation of these are beautiful and will seriously impress your guests. It's everything in one—veggies, protein and a salad. And oh, that carrot ginger dressing—yum!

SERVES 2

TERIYAKI PINEAPPLE CHICKEN WITH ASPARAGUS
IN A PINEAPPLE BOWL

PREPARE THE PINEAPPLE

Scoop out the pineapple from each half. Discard the core, and cut the edible pineapple into chunks.

PREPARE THE TERIYAKI CHICKEN

Season chicken thighs with salt and pepper and cook in a skillet over medium-high heat for 2 to 3 minutes, then flip and cook for 1 to 2 more minutes. Turn the heat to medium, then add teriyaki sauce, garlic, pineapple chunks and asparagus. Cover and cook for an additional 3 to 4 minutes, or until chicken is thoroughly cooked.

MAKE CARROT GINGER DRESSING

While the chicken is cooking, add carrots, vinegar, soy sauce, lemon juice, garlic, ginger, oil, salt and pepper to a food processor. Pulse to combine.

ASSEMBLE

Add some of the dressing to the mixed salad greens and tomatoes, and lightly toss together.

To serve, equally divide the salad mixture into each pineapple bowl. Top with the chicken mixture and serve.

---

1 ripe pineapple, cut in half lengthwise

TERIYAKI CHICKEN

2 boneless, skinless chicken thighs

½ teaspoon salt

¼ teaspoon freshly ground pepper

¼ cup teriyaki sauce

1 clove garlic, minced

8 fresh Michigan asparagus spears, cut into 2-inch pieces

CARROT GINGER DRESSING

2 cups shredded carrots

2 tablespoons rice wine vinegar

2 tablespoons soy sauce

Juice of 1 lemon

2 cloves garlic

1 tablespoon fresh ginger, peeled and chopped

¼ cup olive oil

¼ teaspoon salt

¼ teaspoon freshly ground pepper

2 cups mixed salad greens

¼ cup cherry tomatoes

NOTE

Rinse and dry the outside of the pineapple before cutting.

My grandparents were very important to me. I got my love of cooking from my Grandma Betty, and I grew up learning all about agriculture on my Grandpa Norm's farm. I remember the funniest things about them, including the fact that my grandpa ate a spinach salad every single day of his life for lunch. My grandma, on the other hand, would eat cheeseburgers. I know Grandpa Norm would love this bacon-laden spinach salad, especially since it has fresh fruit on it.

SERVES 2 (LARGE SALADS) or 4 (SMALL SALADS)

STRAWBERRY FETA SPINACH SALAD

CANDIED WALNUTS

- ¼ cup sugar
- ¼ teaspoon cinnamon
- ⅛ teaspoon salt
- ½ cup chopped walnuts

- 4 strips thick-cut bacon

WARM BACON STONE GROUND MUSTARD DRESSING

- 2 tablespoons stone ground mustard
- ⅓ cup red wine vinegar
- 2 tablespoons honey
- ¼ teaspoon salt
- ¼ teaspoon freshly ground pepper

- 5 ounces baby spinach
- ¼ cup crumbled feta
- 1 cup sliced strawberries

MAKE CANDIED WALNUTS

In a small skillet, add sugar, cinnamon, salt and walnuts. Cook over low heat, constantly stirring until all sugar has dissolved and walnuts are thoroughly coated. Pour walnuts onto a parchment paper-lined baking sheet. Let cool.

PREPARE BACON

In a medium skillet, add bacon and cook over medium heat for 7 to 9 minutes, or until done. Remove bacon with a slotted spoon and place on a paper towel to drain. Roughly chop bacon and set aside.

MAKE WARM BACON STONE GROUND MUSTARD DRESSING

With the skillet on medium-low heat, whisk the remaining bacon fat together with mustard, vinegar, honey, salt and pepper. Scrape up any remaining bacon bits and let simmer. Remove from heat and cover to keep warm.

ASSEMBLE

Add spinach to salad bowls. Add bacon, feta and sliced strawberries. (Add blueberries when in season.) Drizzle warm dressing over greens and top with candied walnuts. Serve immediately.

Morel mushrooms are hard to find. We get them once a year here in Michigan, and when we do, I love to make all kinds of different things with them. My kids' favorite is this risotto. I always make extra and, before even serving, I hide some in the fridge so I can make arancini balls the next day. If you can't find fresh morels, buy dried and reconstitute them.

SERVES 6

SPRING MOREL RISOTTO
WITH ASPARAGUS & PEAS

Add chicken stock to a saucepan and keep warm over medium-low heat.

Add oil, butter and onion to a deep pot over medium heat. Cook until onion is translucent, about 3 minutes. Add mushrooms and continue cooking for another 3 minutes, then add garlic, salt and pepper. (Make sure to brown the mushrooms for a few minutes before adding salt, because the salt will pull the moisture out of mushrooms. Browning the mushrooms before adding salt helps keep the integrity of the mushrooms throughout the cooking process.)

Next, add arborio rice. Cook for 2 to 3 minutes, then add wine. When the rice has absorbed most of the liquid, add 1 cup of chicken stock. Continually stir the rice and liquid. Repeat with more stock every time the liquid has absorbed, until the rice is cooked al dente. (The risotto should be firm and creamy, not mushy. This should take approximately 30 minutes.)

ASSEMBLE

Turn the heat to low, then add peas, asparagus and Parmesan. Continue to stir until the cheese has melted. Add extra stock, if the risotto is too thick. Garnish with fresh parsley or chives, and serve warm.

- 5 to 6 cups chicken stock
- 2 tablespoons olive oil
- 2 tablespoons butter
- ½ cup chopped onion
- 1 pound clean morel mushrooms, or any combination of your favorite mushrooms (cut into bite-size pieces, if large)
- 2 cloves garlic, minced
- ½ teaspoon salt, extra for tasting
- ¼ teaspoon freshly ground pepper, extra for tasting
- 1⅔ cup arborio rice
- ¾ cup dry white wine
- 1 cup fresh peas, washed and shelled (or thawed frozen peas)
- 2 cups cut-up fresh or frozen Michigan asparagus, blanched
- ⅔ cup grated Parmesan cheese
- Fresh parsley or chives, for garnish

NOTE

Substitute fresh morel mushrooms with dried morel or porcini mushrooms. Simply reconstitute the dried mushrooms in the warm chicken stock for 20 to 30 minutes, then add them to the recipe.

Morel mushrooms must be thoroughly rinsed clean, while all other mushrooms simply need a damp cloth to wipe away any dirt.

This recipe is special to me for several reasons. Every year, the only thing my mother-in-law wanted for her birthday was a decades-old dessert that had pretzels, cream cheese, cool whip and strawberry Jello. I took that recipe and made it my own, adding a recipe close to my heart—rhubarb. My Grandma Mildred grew up with a huge rhubarb garden. Rhubarb by itself can be bitter, so I've paired it with sweet strawberries and chocolate. The flavor is just amazing.

SERVES 8

RHUBARB & STRAWBERRY PRETZEL CRUMBLE

RHUBARB & STRAWBERRY FRUIT FILLING

- 3 cups fresh rhubarb, washed and cut into bite-size pieces
- 5 cups fresh strawberries, hulled and halved
- ⅔ cup sugar
- Juice & zest of 1 lemon
- ¼ teaspoon freshly ground pepper
- 3 tablespoons cornstarch
- ⅓ cup apple juice

CHOCOLATE PRETZEL CRUMBLE

- 1 sleeve chocolate graham crackers (about 1⅓ cup ground)
- 4 ounces pretzels (about 1 cup crushed)
- ½ cup brown sugar
- ½ cup flour
- ¼ teaspoon salt
- 2 sticks cold butter, cubed

Freshly whipped cream or ice cream, to serve

NOTE

Always taste the fruit raw before cooking, and adjust the sugar accordingly.

Don't have a pastry cutter? Use a large serving fork instead.

Preheat oven to 350°F.

MAKE FRUIT FILLING

In a large bowl, mix together rhubarb, strawberries, sugar, lemon juice, zest and pepper. Dissolve cornstarch in apple juice and pour over the fruit; gently toss together.

MAKE CHOCOLATE PRETZEL CRUMBLE

In a food processor, grind graham crackers until well-ground, then place in a large mixing bowl. Next, grind pretzels in a food processor and pulse to combine. (Don't grind pretzels into a fine grind—keep some texture to them.) Add the crushed pretzels, brown sugar, flour and salt to the graham crackers in the mixing bowl. Mix together, then cut in butter with a pastry cutter.

ASSEMBLE

Add fruit filling to a 9-by-13-inch baking dish. Evenly spread crumble on top of fruit. Cover with aluminum foil and bake for 25 minutes, then remove foil and bake for an additional 25 to 30 minutes.

Serve warm with a dollop of whipped cream or a scoop of ice cream.

BURGERS & SAMMIES
FOR BOATING SEASON

Burgers are my claim to fame, so to speak. But trust me when I say it didn't happen overnight. I didn't grow up grilling, but knew that if I could learn to fly a plane, I could learn to grill. I slowly got into it by making frozen patties, but my burger game changed dramatically with a meat grinder. Now I have a huge commercial-grade meat grinder in my kitchen. People who know me don't bring bottles of wine over to my house as hostess gifts—they bring slabs of meat! When people see the three huge grills and all the grinding equipment at my house, they instantly think it's my husband's stuff. Perhaps my heels, makeup and blonde hair don't help my case, but this girly-girl happens to be the meat butcher, grinder and grill master of our house!

I cannot stress what a difference it makes to grind your own meat. But if that's not your thing, buy 80/20 ground chuck, which fulfills my Grandpa Norm's saying, "Fat is flavor!" I'm a burger purist in that I almost always use beef and not turkey or chicken. We don't have burgers every day, so I believe that when you do, you should have a DAMN good one.

RUSSIAN HORSEY SLAW

½ cup mayonnaise

2 tablespoons ketchup

1 tablespoon Horseradish Sauce (recipe below in note) or 1 tablespoon prepared horseradish

2 tablespoons apple cider vinegar

1½ tablespoons sugar

¼ teaspoon celery seeds

¼ teaspoon salt

2 cups shredded green cabbage

½ cup shredded purple cabbage

½ cup shredded carrots

PATTIES

1½ pounds freshly ground chuck (80/20)

1 tablespoon dill relish or minced dill pickle

1 tablespoon Worcestershire sauce

1 teaspoon caraway seeds

Kosher salt

Fresh ground black pepper

½ pound thinly sliced pepper-crusted pastrami

4 slices cheddar cheese

4 slices Swiss cheese

4 hamburger buns, split

½ cup dill pickle chips

NOTE

To make your own Horseradish Sauce: combine ⅓ cup freshly grated horseradish, 2 teaspoons dijon mustard, 1 tablespoon white vinegar, ¾ teaspoon salt and 1 tablespoon water in a food processor. Pulse until thoroughly combined.

One of my favorite sandwiches in the whole world is pastrami loaded with slaw and Russian dressing on rye bread with caraway seeds. So, of course, this burger had to have all of those elements. I freshly grate my own horseradish sauce. It's so good—and it clears out your sinuses!

SERVES 4

PEPPER-CRUSTED PASTRAMI BURGERS

MAKE SLAW

In a large bowl, whisk together all slaw ingredients except the cabbages and carrots. Once slaw sauce is well-incorporated, mix in cabbages and carrots. Cover and refrigerate until ready to assemble burgers.

MAKE PATTIES

Prepare grill for direct cooking over medium-high heat.

In a large bowl, gently mix together ground chuck, relish or minced dill, Worcestershire sauce and caraway seeds. Gently shape into 4 equal size patties, then depress the centers for even cooking. Season both sides with salt and pepper.

Grill patties over direct heat for 4 to 5 minutes. Turn patties over and place equal amounts of sliced pastrami on each patty, then close the lid and grill for an additional 4 to 5 minutes. During the last minute of cooking, place one slice each of cheddar and Swiss cheese on each patty. During the last minute of cooking, place the buns cut-side down on the outer edges of the grill to toast lightly. Remove buns and patties from grill.

ASSEMBLE

Add an equal amount of pickle chips to each bun bottom. Next add a patty, then top with some slaw and finish with a bun top.

OPTIONAL

Garnish with extra pastrami, cherry tomatoes and pickle chips on a burger skewer.

When I was in college, my favorite burger joint, Mr. Fables in Grand Rapids, was famous for its olive burgers and onion rings. It is my all-time favorite kind of burger—I still dream about it! Although Mr. Fables is no longer in business, I can still remember the sizzle of the burgers on the flat-top grill as you ordered and the taste of those olive burgers. Yum! This is my updated take on that juicy burger.

SERVES 6

MIGHTY MAC OLIVE BURGER

MAKE SAUCE

In a small bowl, mix together cream cheese, Bloody Mary mix, horseradish, ¼ cup chopped olives, olive juice, celery salt and lemon zest. Refrigerate until ready to assemble burgers.

MAKE PATTIES

Prepare grill for direct cooking over medium-high heat.

Gently form the meat into 6 equal patties, then depress the centers for even cooking. Liberally season both sides with salt and pepper.

Grill patties for 10 to 12 minutes, or to desired doneness, turning only once. During the last few minutes of cooking, add equal parts of the remaining chopped olives to each patty, followed by one slice each of provolone and cheddar cheese. Spread garlic butter over all cut sides of buns. During the last minute of cooking, place the buns cut-side down on the outer edges of the grill to toast lightly. Remove buns and patties from grill.

ASSEMBLE

Spread sauce on toasted bun tops and set aside. Add some lettuce to each toasted bun bottom, followed by a patty. Next add some onion slices and a tomato slice. Add toasted bun tops and skewer with a large burger toothpick or a steak knife to hold it all together.

BLOODY MARY OLIVE SAUCE

4 ounces softened cream cheese

1 ounce Brewt's Bloody Mary mix

1 teaspoon prepared horseradish

½ cup chopped green olives with pimentos, divided use

2 teaspoons olive juice

¼ teaspoon celery salt

1 teaspoon fresh lemon zest

PATTIES

2 pounds freshly ground chuck (80/20)

Kosher salt

Freshly cracked black pepper

6 slices provolone cheese

6 slices cheddar cheese

2 tablespoons garlic butter, melted

6 brioche buns, split

Shredded lettuce

Red onion slices

6 tomato slices

SERVES 4

SWEET SMELL OF SUMMER BURGERS
WITH PINEAPPLE SALSA & GUACAMOLE

This is the first burger that got me some culinary attention. At first, I added only the normal burger toppings, like lettuce, tomatoes, pickles, etc. But then one day I decided to add the things I love: pineapple salsa, guacamole and teriyaki sauce. Everyone went crazy for it. Even our former church pastor requests this burger when he visits us from Florida.

TERIYAKI SAUCE
- 1 tablespoon cornstarch
- 1 tablespoon water
- ¼ cup soy sauce
- ¼ cup water
- ¼ cup sugar
- 1 teaspoon minced garlic
- 1 teaspoon minced ginger
- 2 teaspoons roughly chopped thyme

PINEAPPLE SALSA
- 1 cup diced pineapple
- 1 plum tomato, diced
- 2 tablespoons minced red onion
- ⅛ cup roughly chopped cilantro
- 1 clove garlic, minced
- ¼ teaspoon salt
- ¼ teaspoon pepper

GUACAMOLE
- 2 avocados, halved, peeled and seeded
- 2 cloves garlic, minced
- 1 teaspoon grated jalapeño
- Juice of 1 lime
- ½ teaspoon ground cumin
- 1 teaspoon celery salt
- ½ teaspoon freshly ground pepper

PATTIES
- 1½ pounds ground chuck (80/20)
- ¼ cup soy sauce
- Kosher salt
- Freshly ground pepper

- 4 slices Swiss cheese
- 4 brioche buns, split
- 1 cup arugula or mixed greens

MAKE SAUCE

Whisk together cornstarch and water, and set aside. Place all remaining ingredients in a small saucepan and cook over medium heat until sugar dissolves. Whisk in cornstarch-and-water mixture and cook until it starts to thicken. Reduce heat to low and cook for 4 to 5 minutes, then remove from heat. Set aside until ready to assemble burgers.

MAKE SALSA

Add all salsa ingredients to a bowl, then gently fold together. Set aside until ready to assemble burgers.

MAKE GUACAMOLE

Add avocados to a bowl and mash until desired consistency. Fold in all remaining guacamole ingredients and set aside until ready to assemble burgers.

MAKE PATTIES

Prepare grill for direct cooking over medium-high heat.

Combine ground chuck and soy sauce in a large bowl, handling as little as possible to avoid compacting the meat. Divide the mixture into 4 equal portions and form to shape patties, then depress the centers for even cooking. Sprinkle both sides with salt and pepper.

Place patties on the grill, cover and cook, turning only once, about 5 minutes per side for medium. During the last few minutes of grilling, add a cheese slice to each patty. During the last minute of cooking, place the buns cut-side down on the outer edges of the grill to toast lightly. Remove buns and patties from grill.

ASSEMBLE

Top each bun bottom with some arugula, followed by a patty. Drizzle some teriyaki sauce over each patty, then add some salsa and guacamole. Finish with bun tops.

NOTE

GLUTEN-FREE VERSION: Use coconut aminos in place of soy sauce, and substitute lettuce leaves or a gluten-free bun for brioche bun.

VEGETARIAN VERSION: Use a portobello mushroom in place of meat.

VEGAN VERSION: Use agave nectar in place of sugar; use coconut aminos in place of soy sauce; use a portobello mushroom in place of meat; use vegan cheese slice or omit the cheese; use lettuce leaves or vegan hamburger buns in place of brioche buns.

This burger features my famous jalapeño onion popper. Onion rings and jalapeño poppers are a match made in burger heaven, and are meant to be combined. I was chosen to represent our Detroit Lions on a Rachael Ray Show show called "Fantasy Foodball," and this was the burger that I made. Go Lions!

SERVES 4

DEFEND THE DEN BURGERS
TOPPED WITH JALAPEÑO ONION POPPERS & ZESTY SAUCE

ZESTY SAUCE

- ¼ cup mayonnaise
- ¼ cup barbecue sauce
- 1 tablespoon prepared horseradish
- 4 slices thick-cut bacon, cut in half (8 pieces)

JALAPEÑO ONION POPPERS

(SEE OPPOSITE PAGE)

PATTIES

- 1½ pounds ground chuck (80/20)
- 2 tablespoons soy sauce
- Kosher salt
- Freshly ground pepper
- 4 slices cheddar cheese
- 4 hamburger buns, split
- ¾ cup shredded lettuce
- 8 dill pickle slices
- 4 slices tomato
- 2 tablespoons barbecue sauce

JALAPEÑO ONION POPPERS

SERVES 8 TO 10

- Peanut or canola oil (for frying)
- 4 ounces cream cheese
- 3 tablespoons shredded cheddar cheese
- 1 tablespoon chopped jalapeño
- 1 sweet onion, peeled and cut into 8 to 10 (½-inch thick) slices
- ½ cup flour
- ¼ teaspoon House Seasoning (page 96)
- 1 teaspoon kosher salt, divided
- 1 egg
- ½ cup milk
- 1 cup panko breadcrumbs, divided use

Preheat oven to 375°F, and prepare grill for direct cooking over medium-high heat.

MAKE SAUCE

Add mayonnaise, barbecue sauce and horseradish to a small bowl and mix well. Cover and refrigerate until ready to assemble the burgers.

PREPARE BACON

Place bacon on a slotted or parchment paper-lined pan and cook in the preheated oven for 17 to 20 minutes, or until crispy. Lay bacon on paper towels to drain.

MAKE PATTIES

In a large bowl, gently mix together ground chuck and soy sauce. Form the meat into 4 equal patties that are slightly larger in circumference than the bun, then depress the centers for even cooking. Liberally salt and pepper both sides of patties.

Grill patties for 10 to 12 minutes for medium, turning only once. Add 2 bacon strips and a slice of cheese to each patty during the last two minutes of cooking, making sure the cheese is thoroughly melted. During the last minute of cooking, place the buns cut-side down on the outer edges of the grill to toast lightly. Remove buns and patties from grill.

ASSEMBLE

Spread sauce over all cut sides of buns. Starting with the bun bottom, add shredded lettuce, pickle chips and a tomato slice, followed by a patty. Next add an onion popper, then drizzle some barbecue sauce over it. Finish with the bun top.

PREPARE ONION POPPERS

HEAT OIL

Heat a large, heavy pot filled 2 to 3 inches deep with oil to 350°F.

MAKE ONION POPPERS

In a small bowl, mix together cream cheese, cheddar cheese and jalapeños. Next add equal portions of the cream cheese mixture to the inside of the onion slices, then freeze for 10 minutes or until firm.

PREPARE DREDGE

Set up a dredging station with 3 shallow dishes (pie plates work great). Mix flour, House Seasoning and ½ teaspoon salt in the first dish. Beat egg and milk together in the second dish. Place panko in the third dish. One at a time, dredge onion poppers in the flour mixture, then in the egg mixture, then in the panko.

FRY ONION POPPERS

Carefully add onion slices to the hot oil, making sure they do not clump together. Fry for 3 to 4 minutes, turning as needed until crisp and golden-brown. Drain on paper towels. Sprinkle the remaining ½ teaspoon of salt over poppers while hot.

I entered this burger into an online contest with the New York City Wine & Food Festival using the hashtag #NYCWFFdish, and it won! This recipe came from my love of combining chipotle and cherry flavors. They're just a delicious pairing, and complement one another perfectly. I also love mimosas—who doesn't?—so I added that flavor to the peach salsa. So many bold flavors come together for a winning burger.

SERVES 4

SHAKIN' CHIPOTLE CHERRY BURGERS

WITH PEACH MIMOSA SALSA & ADOBO AVOCADO AIOLI ON PRETZEL BUNS

CHERRY CHIPOTLE CHEESE

- 2 tablespoons softened butter
- 1 tablespoon adobo sauce
- ¼ cup fresh black sweet cherries, pitted and chopped
- ½ cup shredded cheddar cheese

PEACH MIMOSA SALSA

- 2 ripe peaches, peeled, pitted and diced
- 2 plum tomatoes, diced
- 2 tablespoons diced red onion
- 2 tablespoons coarsely chopped fresh cilantro
- 1 clove garlic, finely minced
- 1 tablespoon white balsamic vinegar
- 1 ounce sparkling wine or cherry harvest wine

ADOBO AVOCADO AIOLI

- 1 ripe avocado, peeled and seeded
- 1 canned chipotle chili in adobo sauce
- 1 tablespoon freshly squeezed lime juice
- ¼ cup mayonnaise
- ¼ cup sour cream
- 1 clove garlic
- ¼ teaspoon cumin
- ½ teaspoon celery salt
- ½ teaspoon ground pepper

PATTIES

- 1½ pounds ground chuck (80/20)
- Kosher salt
- Freshly ground black pepper

- 4 slices Swiss cheese
- 4 pretzel buns, split
- Mixed salad greens

PREPARE CHEESE

Add all cheese ingredients to a bowl and mix well. Set aside until ready to stuff patties.

MAKE SALSA

Combine all salsa ingredients in a nonreactive bowl. Toss to combine, then cover and refrigerate until ready to assemble burgers.

MAKE AIOLI

Combine all aioli ingredients in a food processor and process until well-blended. Transfer to a bowl, then cover and refrigerate until ready to assemble burgers.

MAKE PATTIES

Prepare grill for direct cooking over medium-high heat.

Gently form ground chuck into 8 thin patties. Add a tablespoon of cheese mixture to the center of 4 patties. Top each with another patty and seal the edges, then sprinkle both sides with salt and pepper.

Grill patties over direct heat for approximately 5 minutes on each side, or to desired doneness. During the last few minutes of cooking, place one slice of Swiss cheese on each patty. During the last minute of cooking, place the buns cut-side down on the outer edges of the grill to toast lightly. Remove buns and patties from grill.

ASSEMBLE

Spread aioli over all cut sides of pretzel buns. Top each bun bottom with a patty, then add mixed greens. Top greens with salsa mixture and finish with bun tops.

NOTE

When cherries aren't in season, feel free to substitute with dried cherries.

These Peach Habanero Mini Burgers are great to make in the summer and early fall when peaches are ripe in Michigan. I love the combination of sweet and spicy, and these are perfect for a summer patio party. Keep extra Bibb or butter lettuce leaves handy and let your guests choose to make mini burgers or a lettuce wrap.

SERVES 12 (SLIDERS) or 6 (BURGERS)

PEACH HABANERO MINI BURGERS

MAKE SAUCE

Add all Peach Habanero Sauce ingredients to a food processor and process until well blended. Set aside.

MAKE PATTIES

Prepare grill for direct cooking over medium-high heat.

In a large bowl, gently mix together ground chuck and soy sauce. Form the meat into 12 equal slider patties (or 6 burger patties), then depress the centers for even cooking. Season both sides with salt and pepper.

Grill patties for 4 to 5 minutes with the grill lid closed as much as possible. Flip patties and grill for 3 to 4 more minutes, depending on your desired doneness. During the last minute of cooking, place buns cut-side down and lightly toast. Remove buns and patties from grill, and lightly tent with foil until ready to assemble.

ASSEMBLE

On each bun bottom, add some lettuce leaves and top with a patty. Next add a tomato slice and some onion slices. Drizzle some Peach Habanero Sauce over onions and tomatoes, then add bun tops.

NOTE

When peaches aren't in season, feel free to substitute with mangoes or pineapple.

PEACH HABANERO SAUCE

4 ripe peaches, peeled and seeded

1 clove garlic

1 habanero, seeded

1 tablespoon freshly squeezed lime juice

¼ cup honey

¼ cup rice wine vinegar

PATTIES

2 pounds freshly ground chuck (80/20)

3 tablespoons soy sauce

Kosher salt

Freshly ground pepper

12 slider buns, split, or 6 hamburger buns

2 cups butter or Bibb lettuce leaves

12 slices heirloom tomatoes (similar to bun size)

½ cup thinly sliced red onions

TIP

How to Grind Meat:
My favorite meat to use for burgers is a combination of chuck, short rib and brisket. Keep the ratio of meat to fat around 80 percent lean meat to 20 percent fat. Add meat to a cutting board and cut into 2-inch cubes. Lay meat cubes on a baking sheet, then place in freezer for 10 to 15 minutes. Add meat grinding attachment to a stand mixer using the coarse grinding plate. Once the beef is very cold, but not frozen, add the cubed meat to the hopper and turn the mixer on to medium speed. Press the cubes down the chute until all the meat is freshly ground. Form into patties and refrigerate until ready to grill.

SERVES 4

CROISSANT CROQUE-MADAME BURGERS

Who says burgers aren't a breakfast food? If I were in charge, I'd eat a burger for breakfast every day. My daughter Ariana studied abroad for a semester in college, and, after a stint in Paris, came home obsessed with buttery croissants. She also loves eggs on a burger, so I came up with this recipe to incorporate both.

MAPLE DIJON BÉCHAMEL

- 2 tablespoons butter
- 2 tablespoons flour
- ½ cup milk
- ⅛ teaspoon salt
- ⅛ teaspoon pepper
- 2 tablespoons maple syrup
- ¼ cup Dijon mustard, divided use
- 1 cup Gruyere cheese, grated, divided use

PATTIES

- 1 pound freshly ground chuck (80/20)
- ½ pound hot Italian sausage, casings removed
- Kosher salt
- Freshly ground pepper

LEMON-PEPPER ASPARAGUS

- 8 asparagus spears, 4 to 5 inches long
- ½ tablespoon avocado oil
- ½ teaspoon lemon-pepper seasoning

EGGS

- 1 tablespoon butter
- 4 eggs
- Kosher salt
- Freshly ground pepper

- 4 ounces thinly sliced deli ham
- 4 slices Swiss cheese
- 4 croissants, split in half lengthwise

MAKE BÉCHAMEL

Whisk together butter and flour in a saucepan and cook for 2 to 3 minutes. Whisk in milk, salt, pepper, maple syrup and half of the Dijon. Continue to whisk until the sauce thickens, about 4 to 5 minutes, then add half of the Gruyere and let melt. Remove from heat and set aside.

MAKE PATTIES

Preheat grill for direct cooking over medium-high heat.

Gently mix together chuck and sausage in a bowl. Form into 4 equal patties similar in size to the croissants, then depress the centers for even cooking. Generously season both sides with salt and pepper.

Grill patties for 5 to 7 minutes each side, or until thoroughly cooked. *(Note: I normally like my burgers medium-rare, but since these have pork in them, they need to be thoroughly cooked.)* During the last few minutes of grilling, add a dollop of béchamel to each patty, followed by a ham slice and a Swiss cheese slice. Top each cheese slice with another dollop of béchamel and equal amounts of the remaining Gruyere. Cover grill and let cheeses melt. Remove from heat, then tent patties with aluminum foil.

PREPARE ASPARAGUS

Drizzle asparagus with avocado oil, and season with lemon-pepper seasoning. Grill for 4 to 5 minutes.

PREPARE EGGS

Heat butter in a nonstick skillet over medium-high heat. Break eggs into skillet, one at a time. Turn heat to low and cook until edges start to turn white. Add 1 tablespoon of water, cover and cook until whites are completely cooked and yolks are thickened. Remove from heat, then season with salt and pepper.

ASSEMBLE

Spread the remaining Dijon over the cut side of the croissants. Starting with the croissant bottom, add a patty and two asparagus spears. Next add an egg and finish with the croissant top.

NOTE

Substitute lemon-pepper asparagus with pickled asparagus, if you want an acidic touch to this burger. Both options are delicious!

This is my take on a grilled cheese, a BLT and a wedge salad—but all on one plate. I dare anyone not to love this sandwich.

SERVES 4

BUFFALO CHICKEN GRILLED CHEESE / WEDGE BLT

4 slices bacon, chopped

4 romaine lettuce leaves, same length as bread

¼ cup Blue Cheese Dressing (page 180)

1 Roma tomato, seeded and diced

2 tablespoons blue cheese crumbles

1 cup rotisserie chicken, skin removed and shredded

⅛ cup finely diced celery

¼ cup Buffalo wing sauce

½ stick butter, softened

8 slices good-quality bread

8 slices Colby jack or American cheese

Celery leaves, for garnish (optional)

MAKE WEDGE BLT

Add chopped bacon to a skillet and cook over medium-high heat until bacon is almost crisp. Remove bacon with slotted spoon and place it on a paper towel to drain.

Add romaine leaves to a plate, and evenly top them with blue cheese dressing, diced tomato, blue cheese crumbles and bacon. Refrigerate until ready to assemble.

In a mixing bowl, toss together chicken, celery and Buffalo wing sauce. Set aside.

MAKE GRILLED CHEESE

Lay out all bread slices on a clean, flat surface. Evenly butter one side of each bread slice, then flip over. Add one cheese slice to the unbuttered side of each bread slice. Evenly distribute the chicken mixture to 4 slices of bread, then top with the other 4 slices, cheese-side down. You now have 4 sandwiches, butter-sides up and ready to cook.

Heat a large griddle pan over medium heat.

Add sandwiches to griddle pan and cook for 3 to 4 minutes each side. Make sure that the cheese is melted. Remove from heat. (If you don't have a large griddle pan, you can use a skillet and cook one or two at a time.)

ASSEMBLE

Start with one grilled cheese sandwich and top with two of the blue cheese-topped romaine lettuce leaves, side by side. Then top with another grilled cheese sandwich. Repeat the process for the other two sandwiches. Skewer both sides of the sandwiches and cut in half.

OPTIONAL

Drizzle on more Buffalo sauce, and add blue cheese crumbles and celery leaves to garnish.

NOTE

If you want to make your own buffalo wing sauce, simply melt butter and add hot sauce (2 parts hot sauce to 1 part butter).

This is the burger that first put me on TV. I made these burgers with all the condiments labeled for my friend Lauren's surprise 40th birthday party. The host of the party happened to be a producer for a Grand Rapids lifestyle show, and, after seeing everyone rave about the burgers, invited me to do a grilling segment for a Fourth of July special. I love the freshness of this burger, and how you get a cold caprese salad and warm burger in every bite.

SERVES 6

CAPRESE BURGERS
WITH PISTACHIO PESTO & BLUEBERRY BALSAMIC DRIZZLE

MAKE BALSAMIC DRIZZLE

In a medium saucepan, add vinegar, blueberries and sugar. Cook over medium-high heat for 10 to 12 minutes, or until mixture reduces by half. Remove from heat and set aside.

MAKE PESTO

Place all pesto ingredients in a food processor and process until well-blended. Set aside.

MAKE PATTIES

Prepare the grill for direct cooking over medium-high heat.

Gently shape ground chuck into 6 patties of equal size and thickness (or 12 small sliders). With your thumb or the back of a spoon, make a shallow indentation about 1 inch wide in the center of each patty. Cover and refrigerate until ready to grill.

Grill patties over direct medium-high heat, with the lid closed as much as possible, for 4 to 5 minutes. Turn patties over and grill an additional 4 to 5 minutes. During the last minute of cooking, place the buns cut-side down on the outer edges of the grill to toast lightly. Remove buns and patties from grill.

ASSEMBLE

Spread pesto over all cut sides of buns. On each bun bottom, add equal amounts of frisee and a patty. Top each patty with a tomato slice, followed by a mozzarella slice. Drizzle balsamic over mozzarella, then add bun tops.

BLUEBERRY BALSAMIC DRIZZLE

1 cup balsamic vinegar

½ cup freshly mashed blueberries

¼ cup brown sugar

PISTACHIO PESTO

2 cups fresh basil leaves

2 tablespoons pistachio nuts

2 cloves garlic

½ cup olive oil

½ cup grated Parmesan cheese

PATTIES

2 pounds freshly ground chuck (80/20)

Kosher salt

Freshly ground pepper

6 hamburger buns, split

6 (¼-inch) slices heirloom tomatoes

6 (¼-inch) slices fresh mozzarella

1½ cups frisee lettuce

NOTE

When blueberries aren't in season, feel free to substitute with strawberries, cherries or any seasonal fruit.

SLAW

2 tablespoons mayo

1 tablespoon adobo sauce

1 tablespoon rice wine vinegar

1 teaspoon sugar

1 cup thinly sliced red cabbage

1 peach, peeled, pitted and diced

¼ cup diced tomatoes

2 tablespoons chopped scallions

DEEP-FRIED AVOCADO

Peanut or vegetable oil, for frying

1 cup flour

1 cup Michigan craft beer

2 teaspoons salt, divided use

1 ripe avocado, halved, peeled, pitted and sliced into 8 slices

1 teaspoon granulated garlic

1 teaspoon cumin

1 tablespoon freshly grated Parmesan

2 tablespoons butter, softened

4 slices buttermilk bread

4 slices provolone

¼ cup arugula

NOTE

This is great as a grilled cheese sandwich, but it also can be made into a taco. Simply add the ingredients to some corn or flour tortillas instead of using bread.

Did you know that Michigan has its very own Gold Coast? We have 300 miles along Lake Michigan that is home to beautiful beaches and sweeping sand dunes. Michigan is also known for its craft breweries. Grand Rapids takes the title of Beer City, USA. Bite into this grilled cheese and you'll have a taste of our Gold Coast. The beer-battered avocado is crunchy on the outside yet creamy on the inside. It's the perfect combination with the cool and crisp peach slaw and peppery arugula.

SERVES 2

GOLD COAST GRILLED CHEESE
BEER-BATTERED AVOCADO GRILLED CHEESE WITH CHIPOTLE PEACH SLAW

MAKE SLAW

In a small bowl, whisk together mayo, adobo sauce, vinegar and sugar. Fold in cabbage, diced peach, tomatoes and scallions. Cover and refrigerate until ready to assemble, or up to 1 week.

MAKE DEEP-FRIED AVOCADO

Add oil to a deep skillet or deep fryer, and bring temperature to 350°F.

In a medium bowl, whisk together flour, beer and 1 teaspoon of salt. Sprinkle avocado slices with garlic, cumin and Parmesan. Dredge avocado slices in the flour mixture, then carefully add the slices to the hot oil. Cook for 2 to 3 minutes each side, or until golden brown. Lay on a paper towel-lined plate and sprinkle with remaining salt while hot.

ASSEMBLE

Heat a large skillet to medium heat. Butter one side of each bread slice, then place buttered sides of bread down into the skillet. Add 1 slice of provolone to the top of each bread slice in the skillet, and cook for 1 minute. On 2 of the bread slices, evenly distribute arugula, avocado slices and slaw. Top with the other 2 bread slices and cook for 2 to 3 minutes, then flip. Cook for 1 to 2 more minutes, or until cheese is melted and bread is golden brown.

This recipe carries the name of my first blog—Boating, Boarding and Burgers. I was invited to do a cooking segment on a TV show, so I had to have a blog. I decided to do 90 burgers in 90 days on the blog in the summer of 2014. That's how this all began! Living on Silver Lake in Michigan, we always go stand-up paddleboarding then eat burgers for dinner. This recipe is our go-to in the summer as the sun was setting after a beautiful day.

SERVES 4

BOATING & BOARDING BURGERS

Preheat oven to 375°F, and preheat grill to medium-high heat.

MAKE SAUCE

Add all Special Sauce ingredients to a small nonreactive bowl. Mix together until well combined. Cover and refrigerate until assembly.

MAKE BURGERS

Place bacon on a slotted or parchment-lined pan and cook in oven for 17 to 20 minutes, or until desired doneness. Lay bacon on paper towels to drain. Set aside until assembly.

Gently form ground chuck into 4 equal patties that are slightly larger in circumference than the bun, then depress the centers for even cooking. Brush patties with canola oil and generously season both sides with salt and pepper. Grill for 10 to 12 minutes for medium doneness, turning only once about halfway through. Add cheese for the last minute or two of cooking, making sure it is thoroughly melted.

ASSEMBLE

Add some sauce to all cut sides of the buns. Starting with the bun bottom, add lettuce, pickles and a burger patty. Next add 2 slices of bacon to each burger and then a tomato slice, finishing with the bun top.

SPECIAL SAUCE

¼ cup mayonnaise

¼ cup ketchup

3 tablespoons dill relish

2 tablespoons horseradish

1 tablespoon grated onion

½ teaspoon sugar

½ teaspoon salt

1 teaspoon freshly ground pepper

BURGERS

8 slices thick-cut maple bacon

1½ pounds ground chuck (80/20)

1 tablespoon canola oil

Kosher salt

Freshly ground pepper

4 slices American or cheddar cheese

4 hamburger buns, split and toasted

Lettuce

Pickle chips

4 tomato slices

BUFFALO CHICKEN QUINOA BURGERS ON AVOCADO TOAST

I know I said I'm a purist and always do beef burgers, but! When you're craving a burger yet want to keep it healthy, make this. It's half quinoa, half lean roasted chicken breast. I like to eat this open-faced in order to cut the extra bread calories, but my husband likes to add another piece of avocado toast on top to make it seem more like a burger. That is up to you. The avocado is rich and creamy, the fresh heirloom tomatoes are so sweet, and the mixed greens add a nice peppery flavor. And when you bite into it, you get a nice crunch from the toasted bread. To top the whole thing off, you get a spicy buffalo sauce.

SERVES 4

PATTIES

- 1 cup cooked red quinoa
- 1 cup shredded rotisserie chicken
- ⅓ cup Italian-style breadcrumbs
- ¼ cup Parmesan cheese, grated
- 2 ounces feta cheese, crumbled
- 1 egg, beaten
- ½ teaspoon granulated garlic
- 1 teaspoon cumin, divided use
- ¾ cup Buffalo wing sauce, divided use
- 2 tablespoons olive oil

AVOCADO TOAST

- 2 avocados, halved, peeled and seeded
- Juice of 1 lime
- 1 clove garlic, minced
- ¼ teaspoon celery salt
- 4 slices wheat nut bread

- 2 cups mixed greens
- 1 heirloom tomato, cut into ¼-inch slices
- ¼ cup cherry tomatoes, halved
- Kosher salt
- Freshly ground pepper
- 2 tablespoons Honey Mustard Red Wine Vinaigrette (page 52)

NOTE

If you want to make your own Buffalo wing sauce, simply melt butter and add hot sauce (2 parts hot sauce to 1 part butter).

Preheat oven to 350°F.

MAKE PATTIES

In a large bowl, add quinoa, chicken, breadcrumbs, cheeses, egg, garlic and half of the cumin and Buffalo sauce. Mix together thoroughly, then gently shape the mixture into 4 equal-size patties. Place patties on a parchment paper-lined baking sheet and bake for 15 minutes.

In a large skillet over medium-high heat, add olive oil. When oil is hot, add patties and sear for 1 minute per side. Remove from heat, and drizzle remaining Buffalo sauce over patties.

PREPARE AVOCADO TOAST

In a small bowl, mash avocados to desired consistency. Stir in remaining cumin, lime juice, garlic and celery salt.

Toast bread to desired crispness.

ASSEMBLE

Spread equal portions of mashed avocado over each slice of toast, then add some mixed greens and the patties. Top each patty with an heirloom-tomato slice and some cherry-tomato halves. Sprinkle with salt and pepper. Garnish with the remaining mixed greens, then drizzle with the vinaigrette.

OPTIONAL

This is an open-faced burger, so top with an additional slice of toast to make a complete burger.

MINERS BEACH FALLS
IN PICTURED ROCKS NATIONAL LAKESHORE

4

SUMMER

Summer is to cherries and blueberries in Michigan as spring is to asparagus. Michigan is the top producer of tart cherries in the country. It's an intense but short season. Seems like every weekend there's a parade or festival in the summer, but the biggest is the National Cherry Festival in Traverse City with all kinds of different bands every night.

I wish I could bottle up the best Michigan summer days, where temperatures hover in the mid 80s thanks to Lake Michigan and our Lake Effect. There's just something about lake life that's just the best! Summers are relaxed with bonfires on the beach, early morning golf tee times and anything and everything to do with water. Basically our entire state is bordered by water—we have the nation's longest freshwater coastline—and more than 11,000 inland lakes! It's only natural, or perhaps mandatory, to get outside and kayak, stand-up paddleboard, climb waterfalls, boat or do anything else on the water.

Michigan is one of the top producers of blueberries in the country. It's a huge summer fruit here, with U-Pick fields everywhere. People on vacation here (and locals!) can pick their own blueberries or go to tons of roadside stands. This cake is so great for any time of day. When we opened our first hotel in Silver Lake, I'd include this cake in the morning breakfast bar for our guests. It was a crowd favorite. The lemon zest is so important in this cake—it brings out the flavors of the blueberries really well.

SERVES 12

BUTTERMILK BLUEBERRY BREAKFAST CAKE

BLUEBERRY CAKE

2 cups flour

2 teaspoons baking powder

½ teaspoon salt

1 stick butter, softened

1¼ cups sugar

2 eggs

1 tablespoon vanilla extract

1 cup buttermilk

Zest of one lemon

2½ cups fresh blueberries, divided use

TOPPING

¼ cup brown sugar

¼ cup sugar

½ cup flour

1 stick cold butter, cut into cubes

Preheat oven to 350°F.

MAKE BLUEBERRY CAKE

In a medium bowl, sift together flour, baking powder and salt. Set aside.

Using an electric stand mixer with a paddle attachment, cream together the softened butter and sugar on high speed until creamy. Turn the mixer to medium-low and slowly add eggs, vanilla and buttermilk. Add the flour mixture and beat until thoroughly combined. Scrape down the sides of the bowl, as necessary.

Gently fold in lemon zest and 2 cups of blueberries. Pour batter into a greased 9-by-13-inch baking dish, then top with the remaining ½ cup of blueberries.

MAKE TOPPING

In a medium bowl, mix together sugars and flour. Using a pastry cutter or a large fork, cut butter into mixture until butter is well-incorporated.

ASSEMBLE

Dollop the crumble topping evenly over the blueberry batter. Bake, uncovered, for 50 to 55 minutes, or until a toothpick inserted into the center comes out clean.

NOTE

Add the zest of 2 lemons for a more pronounced lemon flavor in this cake.

This is one of my family's favorite breakfast dishes. It's also a great way to get kids to eat eggs. Some of our friends claim that their kids don't like eggs, but these delicious egg cups have not failed to please a single one of them. Between the Pillsbury dough, cream cheese and ranch seasoning, you don't even taste the egg. They're very filling, flavorful and great to make ahead and freeze. We grow tons of delicious bell peppers here in Michigan from about July to October, but this recipe is super flexible, so throw in whatever you have.

SERVES 12

CHEESY HAM & PEPPER EGG CUPS

Preheat oven to 375°F.

Unroll dough onto parchment paper, for easy clean-up. In a small bowl, mix together cream cheese and ranch seasoning. Spread evenly over dough. Top with ham and half of the cheese, then roll up into a log. Cut into 12 slices. In a greased 12-cup muffin pan, add one slice of dough to each cup.

In a bowl, whisk together eggs, milk, peppers, salt and pepper. Pour evenly over the dough mixture in each muffin cup. Sprinkle remaining cheese over each egg cup.

Bake for 18 to 22 minutes.

ASSEMBLE

Let cool for 5 minutes before removing cups. Garnish with fresh herbs and serve.

- 1 (8-ounce) can Pillsbury crescent dough sheet
- 4 ounces cream cheese, softened
- 1 tablespoon dry ranch seasoning
- ½ cup cubed ham
- 1 cup shredded cheddar cheese, divided use
- 6 eggs
- 1 cup milk
- ¼ cup diced fresh Michigan bell peppers
- ½ teaspoon salt
- ¼ teaspoon freshly ground pepper
- Fresh herbs, for garnish

NOTE

Give this optional preparation method a try: Cut bell peppers in half, lengthwise, and scoop out the seeds. Place a halved bell pepper, cut-side up, on a baking sheet and add the sliced dough and egg mixture to the inside of it (instead of using a muffin tin). Bake for 25 to 30 minutes. This is a great breakfast-for-dinner idea.

Use any bell peppers that you have. I like to use a combination of peppers for the color contrast.

At the end of summer, we have so much corn that we throw a ton of it, husk-on, into a canoe filled with water and soak it all day. It's almost like brining. Then we grill them and do our take on a low-country boil, without the shrimp.

SERVES 8

CANOE CORN LAKE BAKE

- 3 pounds Michigan potatoes (white, red or purple)
- 1 large onion, peeled and quartered
- 1 tablespoon House Seasoning, plus extra for garnish (see below)
- 2 lemons, halved
- 3 (12-ounce) packages cooked Polish sausage (kielbasa), cut into 3-inch pieces
- 8 ears husked sweet corn, broken in half
- 1 pound fresh green beans, trimmed
- Lemon slices and herbs, for garnish

HOUSE SEASONING

- ¼ cup salt
- 2 tablespoons granulated garlic
- 2 tablespoons granulated onion
- 1 tablespoon freshly ground pepper
- 2 teaspoons smoked paprika

Mix all seasonings together and store in an air-tight container.

MAKE BAKE

Fill a large stock pot ⅔ full with salted water and bring to a boil. Add potatoes, onion, seasoning and lemons, and cook for 10 minutes. Add sausage and corn, and continue to cook for another 10 minutes. Add green beans and cook for 3 to 5 more minutes, or until everything is done. Drain.

ASSEMBLE

Serve with fresh lemons and herbs.

NOTE

House Seasoning can be substituted with Lawry's seasoning salt or Old Bay seasoning.

This recipe is for medium to large potatoes. If you use small potatoes, don't add them in too early. Also, do not cut the potatoes, leave them whole.

This is the best in the entire world. If people are coming over, you absolutely should make this. I use brioche because it has a high butter content. Brioche used to be a little tricky to find but is now even available at Meijer. Because we're wonderfully located in the Fruit Belt, we have amazing cherries, strawberries and blueberries fresh in summer. But use whatever berries you have fresh at that time. I don't recommend using frozen fruit, but if you must, thaw and drain it as much as possible, and add 1 tablespoon of tapioca per cup of fruit.

SERVES 8 to 10

CHERRY-BERRY STUFFED FRENCH TOAST CASSEROLE

FILLING
- 1 (8-ounce) package cream cheese, softened
- 3 tablespoons sugar

EGG MIXTURE
- 6 eggs
- ½ cup half-and-half
- 2 teaspoons vanilla extract
- 1 teaspoon sugar
- ½ teaspoon cinnamon
- ⅛ teaspoon salt

TOPPING
- ¼ cup butter
- ¼ cup brown sugar
- ½ cup fresh blueberries
- 1 teaspoon vanilla extract
- 1 tablespoon corn syrup

- 12 brioche slices, as dry as possible
- 2 cups assorted fresh summer berries and cherries (strawberries, sweet cherries, blueberries, raspberries, blackberries)
- ½ cup pure maple syrup, for garnish
- Fresh mint leaves, for garnish

Preheat oven to 350° F. Spray a 9-by-13-inch baking dish with nonstick cooking spray.

MAKE FILLING

In a medium bowl, beat together cream cheese and sugar until smooth.

MAKE EGG MIXTURE

In a large bowl, whisk together eggs, half-and-half, vanilla, sugar, cinnamon and salt.

MAKE TOPPING

In a small saucepan, heat all topping ingredients together over medium heat until butter is melted and everything is well-incorporated.

ASSEMBLE

Add 6 slices of brioche bread to cover the bottom of the baking dish, then evenly spread the filling over the bread slices. Add 1 cup of the fruit, then add remaining 6 slices of bread. Pour the egg mixture over the entire dish. Make sure the egg mixture gets evenly distributed by gently pressing down on all the bread slices with a spatula or clean hands.

Evenly pour the topping over the egg-soaked bread and bake for 45 to 50 minutes, or until done. Let set up for at least 10 to 15 minutes before serving.

Garnish with the remaining fresh fruit, maple syrup and mint leaves.

NOTE

Use any combination of berries and cherries (strawberries should be hulled and halved; cherries should be pitted and halved before using).

Keep extra maple syrup on the table when serving.

Optional: Adding ½ cup of Cherry Pie Filling (page 117) inside the layers of this dish also is delicious!

Stone fruits like peaches, plums and nectarines are great grilled. It really brings out the caramelization. I like to pair stone fruits with my lime infused icing, which is the ideal balance of sweet and acidic. It's a perfect fruit salad for any meal, and adds a touch of summer's freshness.

SERVES 6 to 8

GRILLED FRUIT SALAD

Preheat grill to medium-high heat.

PREPARE GRILLED FRUIT

In a small bowl, whisk together oil, honey, vinegar, salt and pepper. Brush over halved stone fruit.

Place fruit, cut-side down, on grill. Grill for 3 to 4 minutes on each side.

MAKE ICING

In a small bowl, whisk together powdered sugar, water and the juice of 1 lime.

ASSEMBLE

Add all fruit to a large serving bowl. Top fruit with juice of remaining lime, then drizzle with icing. Garnish with mint leaves.

GRILLED FRUIT

2 tablespoons canola oil

1 tablespoon honey

1 tablespoon cherry balsamic vinegar (or white balsamic)

⅛ teaspoon salt

⅛ teaspoon black pepper

3 fresh peaches, halved and pitted

3 fresh plums, halved and pitted

3 fresh nectarines, halved and pitted

ICING

¼ cup powdered sugar

1 tablespoon water

Juice of 2 limes, divided use

1 cup fresh strawberries, hulled

½ cup fresh blackberries

½ cup fresh raspberries

½ cup fresh sweet cherries, pitted

½ cup fresh blueberries

Fresh mint leaves, for garnish

Garlic scapes are some of my favorites, but they are only available once a year at the end of June. They are the funky, twirly green flower buds of the garlic plant that get cut off to encourage bulb growth. You can eat them just like garlic—even raw—but I like to stuff them in chicken. They taste just like fresh green beans when sautéed and are even great when grilled. If you don't have garlic scapes, just use regular garlic.

SERVES 4

GARLIC SCAPE STUFFED CHICKEN BREAST

- 4 boneless, skinless chicken breasts
- 1 tablespoon House Seasoning (page 96)
- ¼ cup Garlic Scape Pesto (recipe on facing page)
- 8 fresh asparagus spears, trimmed to 5 to 6 inches in length
- 8 fresh garlic scapes
- ¼ cup shredded mozzarella cheese
- 2 tablespoons grated Parmesan cheese
- 2 tablespoons canola oil
- 2 tablespoons butter

Preheat oven to 400°F.

Slice chicken breasts in half, lengthwise, almost all the way through the center, and lay flat. Evenly sprinkle seasoning over both sides of the butterflied chicken breasts. Evenly spread the pesto on the inside of each breast, followed by 2 asparagus spears and 2 garlic scapes. Sprinkle cheeses over top, then roll up each breast. Secure with toothpicks, if necessary.

Melt oil and butter in a cast-iron skillet over medium heat. When the skillet is hot, add the stuffed chicken breasts. Cook for 1 to 2 minutes on each side. (Remove toothpicks, if added, and place chicken seam-side down in skillet.) Transfer skillet to oven and bake for 12 to 15 minutes, or until chicken is completely cooked.

Remove chicken and let rest. Serve with Heirloom Caprese Salad.

NOTE

Add a splash of balsamic vinegar or glaze, red wine vinegar or a squeeze of fresh lemon over this entire dish just before serving.

HEIRLOOM CAPRESE SALAD

3 large heirloom tomatoes, cut into ¾-inch slices

8 ounces fresh mozzarella, sliced ½-inch thick

2 tablespoons Garlic Scape Pesto (recipe below)

Fresh basil leaves, for garnish

ASSEMBLE

Layer tomato and mozzarella slices on a platter. Drizzle pesto over slices and garnish with fresh basil.

GARLIC SCAPE PESTO

1½ cups fresh basil leaves

¼ cup chopped garlic scapes (or 2 cloves garlic)

1 cup olive oil

½ cup grated Parmesan cheese

Juice and zest of 1 lemon

¼ teaspoon salt

⅛ teaspoon freshly ground pepper

ASSEMBLE

Add all pesto ingredients to a food processor and process for 2 to 3 minutes. Scrape down the sides of the processor, as necessary. Taste and add extra salt and pepper, if desired.

Cover and refrigerate any leftover pesto. Pesto will last about 5 to 7 days.

There are so many reasons why you should try this recipe—it's a healthy, kid-friendly snack. It's also a great way to use all that summer zucchini, and it won't break your summer diet. To spice it up, I use a locally made sausage from our grocery store in town, Hansen Foods.

SERVES 4

PEPPERONI PIZZA ZUCCHINI BOATS

- 4 medium zucchini, halved lengthwise
- 1 teaspoon granulated garlic
- 1 tablespoon canola oil
- 1 pound hillbilly sausage (See Note)
- 1 small onion, chopped
- 1 clove garlic, minced
- ½ teaspoon salt
- ¼ teaspoon freshly ground pepper
- 2 tablespoons grated Parmesan cheese
- 1 cup shredded mozzarella cheese, divided use
- 1 cup Homemade Pizza Sauce (page 178)
- ¼ cup pepperoni
- Fresh basil or oregano, for garnish

Preheat oven to 375°F.

MAKE ZUCCHINI BOATS

Using a spoon, scoop out some of the flesh from the inside of each zucchini half (creating a boatlike appearance). Place zucchini boats on a baking sheet and sprinkle the insides with granulated garlic. Transfer zucchini flesh to a cutting board and roughly chop. Set aside.

MAKE FILLING

Add oil, sausage and onion to a skillet, and cook over medium-high heat for 4 to 5 minutes. Then add garlic, chopped zucchini flesh, salt and pepper. Continue to cook for another 4 to 5 minutes. Stir in Parmesan cheese and ½ cup of mozzarella, then remove from the heat.

ASSEMBLE

Using a slotted spoon, spoon the mixture into the zucchini boats. Add the pizza sauce and remaining mozzarella cheese, then top with pepperoni. Bake for 20 to 22 minutes, or until fork-tender.

Garnish with basil or oregano.

NOTE

Slice the zucchini into thin rounds and make pizza bites.

To make hillbilly sausage: add sage, salt, red and black pepper to pork sausage.

Larger is not always better when it comes to zucchini. The small to medium zucchini have more flavor and are less fibrous than larger zucchinis.

GRILLED CHERRY-CHIPOTLE PORK TENDERLOIN
WITH CHERRY SALSA

This is an easy yet impressive recipe for summer if you don't have a lot of time. You can marinate this ahead of time and when you are ready to grill, this dish can be ready in less than 30 minutes. If you're looking for a go-to salsa, this is my favorite recipe, whether or not you have fresh cherries. The adobo sauce is spicy, but brown sugar and cherries tone it down.

SERVES 4

- 1 whole pork tenderloin (approximately 1 pound)

MARINADE

- ½ cup vegetable oil
- ½ cup tart Montmorency cherry juice
- ¼ cup brown sugar
- Juice and zest of 2 limes
- 2 cloves garlic, minced
- 2 tablespoons adobo sauce
- 1 teaspoon salt

CHERRY SALSA

- 6 vine-ripened tomatoes, cored (or 28 ounces canned tomatoes)
- ½ small onion, peeled (¼ cup)
- 1 small jalapeño, trimmed and seeded
- 2 cloves garlic
- ¼ cup fresh cilantro, plus extra for garnish
- 2 tablespoons red wine vinegar
- 2 teaspoons sugar
- 1 teaspoon salt
- ½ teaspoon pepper
- 1 teaspoon House Seasoning (page 96)
- 1 cup sweet cherries, pitted and divided use

NOTE

1 cup sweet cherries = approximately 20 cherries

Salsa makes approximately 3 cups.

Oven-roasting instead of grilling: Heat a cast-iron skillet to medium heat and add marinated pork tenderloin. Cook for 1 minute each side, or until browned, then transfer to oven at 400°F for 20 to 30 minutes.

Trim any fat or silverskin from the pork.

MAKE MARINADE

In a small bowl, mix together all marinade ingredients. Reserve 2 tablespoons of marinade, and pour the rest over the pork tenderloin in a resealable bag. Refrigerate the bag for at least 2 hours, or up to 12.

MAKE SALSA

Add all Cherry Salsa ingredients, except for ½ cup of the sweet cherries, to a food processor. Roughly chop the reserved cherries and set aside. Process the salsa ingredients for 20 to 30 seconds. Pour the salsa into a small bowl, then mix in the remaining chopped cherries. Cover and refrigerate until assembly.

PREPARE PORK

Preheat grill to medium-high heat.

Remove pork from marinade, and discard used marinade. Grill pork for 12 to 15 minutes, turning halfway through. Brush the pork with the reserved 2 tablespoons of marinade while grilling. Remove from grill, lightly tent with foil and let rest for 5 to 10 minutes before slicing. (Internal temperature should reach 145°F for a slight pink inside or up to 160°F for well-done.)

ASSEMBLE

Place pork on a cutting board and cut into desired slices. Sprinkle cut slices with House Seasoning. Drizzle ½ cup Cherry Salsa over pork, and garnish with fresh cilantro.

This is my take on a Michigan cherry salad. At every restaurant in Michigan, you will see a cherry salad on the menu. The basics are dried cherries, salad greens, candied nuts, blue cheese and/or gorgonzola. I like to do the candied cayenne walnuts to add a little sweet heat. We grow spicy Asian greens for a short time here in the summer, but if those aren't available, feel free to substitute your favorite leafy greens. I love this dressing so much that I always keep it on hand.

SERVES 6

MICHIGAN CHERRY SALAD
WITH MAPLE-CAYENNE CANDIED WALNUTS AND CHERRY-BALSAMIC VINAIGRETTE

MAKE MAPLE-CAYENNE CANDIED WALNUTS

Preheat oven to 400°F.

In a small saucepan, add butter, maple syrup, vanilla, sugar, cayenne, salt and walnuts. Cook over medium heat for 3 to 4 minutes. Pour walnuts onto a parchment paper-lined baking sheet and bake for 7 to 9 minutes, or until walnuts are caramelized. Let cool.

PREPARE BACON

In a small skillet, add bacon and cook over medium-high heat for 9 to 11 minutes, or until done but not too crispy. Remove bacon with slotted spoon and place on a paper towel to drain.

MAKE CHERRY-BALSAMIC VINAIGRETTE

In a small bowl, whisk together vinegars, mustard and cherry preserves. Slowly pour in olive oil, continually whisking until everything is well incorporated. Refrigerate until ready to assemble.

ASSEMBLE

Add mixed greens and dried cherries to a large bowl. Add bacon, onion slices and blue cheese crumbles. Drizzle dressing over greens and top with black sweet cherries, when in season. Toss and serve.

MAPLE-CAYENNE CANDIED WALNUTS

- 1 tablespoon butter
- 1 tablespoon Michigan maple syrup
- 1 teaspoon vanilla extract
- 1 tablespoon sugar
- ¼ teaspoon cayenne pepper
- ⅛ teaspoon salt
- 3 ounces chopped walnuts (about ¾ cup)

6 slices thick-cut bacon, chopped

CHERRY-BALSAMIC VINAIGRETTE

- 2 tablespoons balsamic vinegar
- 3 tablespoons rice wine vinegar
- 1 teaspoon Dijon mustard
- ¼ cup cherry preserves
- ¼ cup olive oil

- 16 ounces Asian mixed greens (substitute: any fresh field greens)
- ½ cup dried cherries
- ½ cup thinly sliced red onions
- ½ cup blue cheese crumbles
- Fresh Michigan black sweet cherries, pitted and halved, for garnish (if in season)

Dill pickles are the first thing I ever learned to make. My grandma taught me when I was about 8 years old. I can't count how many pounds of pickles I've made. My grandpa woud bring in 5-gallon buckets full of pickling cucumbers straight from the farm. My grandma and I would get so tired of washing them that at one point we tried to put them in the washing machine on a gentle cycle. It took some of the skin off, so back to hand washing we went. We'd can and can until we ran out of jars. I love to drink the pickle juice out of the jars, so at one point, I remember my grandma locked the cellar where the pickles were stored because she kept finding shriveled cucumbers in empty jars. While my grandma's version would take days, I do a quick dill because I want to eat them quickly.

MAKES 4 PINTS

QUICK DILL PICKLES

- 12 to 14 small pickling cucumbers
- 2 teaspoons coriander seed
- 4 cloves garlic
- 2 teaspoons celery seed
- 2 teaspoons dill seed (use fresh dill seed, when in season)
- 1 tablespoon black peppercorns
- 1 jalapeño, quartered
- 2 cups water
- 2 cups vinegar
- 3 tablespoons salt

Wash and dry cucumbers. Cut off ends and cut into spears.

In the bottom of 4 pint-size jars, add equal amounts of coriander seed, garlic, celery seed, dill seed, peppercorns and jalapeño quarters. Add spears to the jars, keeping them tight but not too tight.

In a saucepan, add water, vinegar and salt. Bring to a boil and allow salt to dissolve. Remove from heat.

Pour vinegar mixture into each jar, leaving a ½-inch space at the top. Cover jars with lids and refrigerate. These quick pickles are great by the next day. Refrigerate up to 3 weeks.

We all love buttery, garlic noodles any time of year. But when you add tons of fresh summer veggies while they are in all their glory, the result is this colorful fan favorite. You can substitute any pasta shape that you like, and, to put this over the top, add bacon!

SERVES 4 to 6

SUMMER VEGGIE PASTA

Bring a large pot of salted water to a boil.

In a large skillet, add oil and heat over medium heat. When the skillet is hot, add zucchini and minced garlic. Cook for 4 to 5 minutes then set aside.

When water is boiling, add pasta and green beans, and cook for 4 minutes. Reserve 1 cup of pasta water, then drain the rest. Add pasta back to the pot, then add butter, granulated garlic and Parmesan cheese. Stir together, adding reserved pasta water a little at a time until creamy. Fold in squash, tomatoes, mozzarella balls and reserved zucchini, then squeeze lemon juice over the entire dish. Serve with fresh summer herbs.

- 2 tablespoons olive oil
- 2 small zucchini, trimmed and cut into ¼-inch pieces
- 2 cloves garlic, minced
- 1 pound angel hair pasta
- 1 pound fresh green beans, trimmed
- ½ cup butter
- ½ teaspoon salt
- ¼ teaspoon freshly ground pepper
- ½ teaspoon granulated garlic
- ½ cup shredded Parmesan cheese
- 2 small yellow summer squash, trimmed and cut into ¼-inch pieces
- 1 cup cherry tomatoes, halved
- 1 (8-ounce) container mini mozzarella balls (bocconcini)
- Juice of 1 lemon
- Fresh summer herbs, for garnish

NOTE

I like my cherry tomatoes raw in this dish, but if you want them warm and softened a bit, add them to the zucchini in the skillet during the last few minutes of cooking.

This is one of my favorite appetizers. I keep the foundation of this crostini super simple with roasted cherry tomatoes and ricotta cheese on garlic toasts. But when I serve it, I add optional toppings on the side, like blue cheese or feta crumbles and thinly sliced medium-rare steak. Throw in some balsamic glaze and heck … that's lunch for me!

SERVES 4 to 6

ROASTED AND TOASTED
TOMATO CROSTINI

- 1 loaf fresh baguette or country bread
- ¼ cup avocado oil, divided use, plus more for drizzling
- 2 cloves garlic
- 1½ pounds cherry tomatoes
- Salt
- Freshly ground black pepper
- 1½ cups ricotta cheese
- Fresh basil leaves or oregano, for garnish
- ¼ cup blue cheese or feta crumbles (optional)

Preheat oven to 425°F.

Cut bread into ½-inch thick slices and place on a baking sheet. Brush bread with 2 tablespoons of oil and bake for 10 to 12 minutes, or until crusty and golden brown. Remove from oven and immediately rub each slice with garlic. Set aside until ready to assemble.

Add tomatoes to a rim-lined baking sheet, lined with foil, and drizzle with 2 tablespoons of oil. Season tomatoes with salt and pepper, then roast for 12 to 15 minutes.

ASSEMBLE

Spread ricotta (about 1 tablespoon) on each slice, and top with roasted tomatoes. Drizzle on remaining oil, then sprinkle with more salt and pepper. Garnish with fresh basil leaves or oregano. Top with blue cheese or feta crumbles, if desired.

NOTE

Jazz this dish up when serving by adding different cheeses and balsamic glazes on the side.

Michigan is known for its cherries, both sweet and tart. We even have the National Cherry Festival in Traverse City every July. Growing up, cherry season was a very special time on the farm. The big, black, sweet cherries were so fun to pick. And the tart cherries were fun to watch because they have to be shaken off the trees. I always loved to ride on the shaker during cherry season. This recipe is great because it has three types of cherries: sweet, tart and dried. They all add a different flavor and texture to this dish. Brownies have a tendency to dry out after a day or so, but not with this recipe. The cherries keep these brownies very moist!

SERVES 12

TRIPLE CHERRY BROWNIES

PREPARE CHERRY PIE FILLING

In a medium saucepan over medium heat, add cherries, cornstarch, sugar, water, almond extract and lemon juice. Cook for 10 to 12 minutes, or until thickened. Remove from the heat and let cool.

PREPARE BROWNIES

Preheat oven to 350°F.

Spray a 9-by-13-inch baking pan with nonstick cooking spray. Prepare the brownie mix, according to the instructions on the box.

ASSEMBLE

Gently fold in the cherry pie filling and cherries, mix thoroughly and pour into the prepared pan. Bake for 35 to 40 minutes, or until a toothpick inserted into the center comes clean.

Garnish with extra cherry pie filling and serve.

CHERRY PIE FILLING

1 cup fresh tart cherries, pitted

2 tablespoons cornstarch

3 tablespoons sugar

3 tablespoons water

¼ teaspoon almond extract

2 tablespoons freshly squeezed lemon juice

BROWNIES

1 (21-ounce) box triple chocolate brownie mix and all ingredients listed on the back (usually eggs, oil and water)

¼ cup black sweet cherries, pitted and halved

2 tablespoons dried cherries

NOTE

If using frozen cherries, let thaw completely. Make sure the cherry filling thickens and cools before adding to brownie mixture.

BIG SABLE POINT LIGHTHOUSE IN LUDINGTON STATE PARK

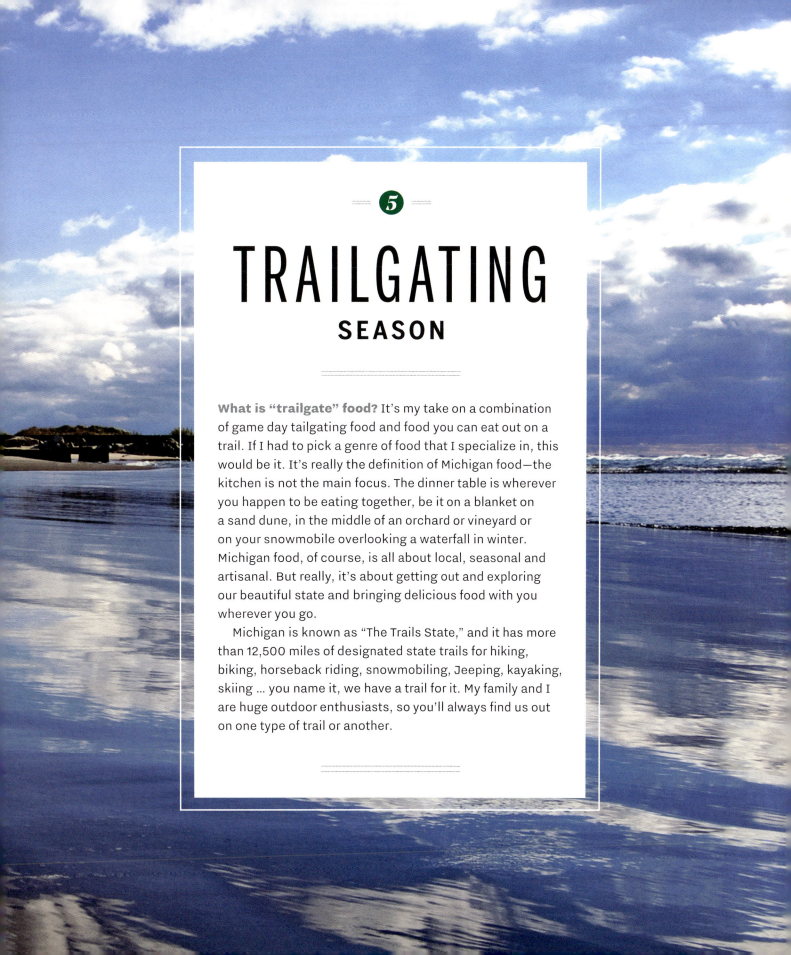

5

TRAILGATING
SEASON

What is "trailgate" food? It's my take on a combination of game day tailgating food and food you can eat out on a trail. If I had to pick a genre of food that I specialize in, this would be it. It's really the definition of Michigan food—the kitchen is not the main focus. The dinner table is wherever you happen to be eating together, be it on a blanket on a sand dune, in the middle of an orchard or vineyard or on your snowmobile overlooking a waterfall in winter. Michigan food, of course, is all about local, seasonal and artisanal. But really, it's about getting out and exploring our beautiful state and bringing delicious food with you wherever you go.

Michigan is known as "The Trails State," and it has more than 12,500 miles of designated state trails for hiking, biking, horseback riding, snowmobiling, Jeeping, kayaking, skiing ... you name it, we have a trail for it. My family and I are huge outdoor enthusiasts, so you'll always find us out on one type of trail or another.

This is a versatile dish that makes for the perfect picnic or trail food. It's not mayonnaise-based, so it won't spoil quickly, and it can be eaten as a salad while you're out on a trail or added to skewers for party food. Or, pair this with sandwich from my Charcuterie Board Picnic (page 124) for a perfectly rounded meal. You know my love of Bloody Marys, so naturally, I incorporate that into this delicious vinaigrette.

SERVES 4

ANTIPASTO SALAD
WITH BLOODY MARY VINAIGRETTE

Cook tortellini al dente, according to the package instructions, then drain and let cool.

In a small bowl, whisk together Bloody Mary mix, red wine vinegar and olive oil until well-incorporated and emulsified.

In a large bowl, add tortellini, artichoke hearts, olives, tomatoes, pepperoncini, mozzarella balls and salami. Gently fold in vinaigrette and toss everything together. Cover and refrigerate for at least 1 hour.

Garnish with fresh basil leaves. Drizzle with balsamic glaze, if desired.

- 1 (10-ounce) package cheese tortellini
- 6 ounces Brewt's Bloody Mary mix
- ¼ cup red wine vinegar
- ¼ cup extra-virgin olive oil
- 1 (14-ounce) can quartered artichoke hearts, drained
- 1 cup medium pitted ripe black olives, drained
- 1 cup cherry tomatoes, halved
- 1 cup pepperoncini peppers
- 8 ounces fresh mozzarella balls
- 8 ounces black pepper salami, cut into bite-size pieces
- Fresh basil leaves, for garnish
- Balsamic glaze (optional)

I love slow cookers, and this is one of my favorite recipes because it can be used as the base for so many things: pulled-pork sandwiches, nachos, tacos … you name it. On game day, set up a pulled-pork bar with buns, tortilla chips, corn tortillas, slaw and all your other favorite condiments.

SERVES 8 to 10

APPLE AND ONION PULLED PORK SANDWICHES & NACHOS

APPLE AND ONION PULLED PORK

- 1 cup ketchup
- 1 cup brown sugar
- ⅔ cup apple cider vinegar
- 1 tablespoon mesquite seasoning
- 1 large onion, thinly sliced
- 1 large apple, peeled, cored and thinly sliced
- 5- to 6-pound bone-in pork shoulder roast

FOR SANDWICHES

- 2 cups Apple and Onion Pulled Pork (recipe above)
- Slaw (page 186)
- Hamburger buns or potato rolls
- Barbecue sauce (optional)

FOR NACHOS

- 1 (16-ounce) bag of tortilla chips
- 2 cups Apple and Onion Pulled Pork (recipe above)
- 2 cups shredded pepper jack cheese
- ½ cup pickled jalapeños
- 1 cup shredded lettuce
- 1 cup diced tomatoes
- ½ cup diced green pepper
- ¼ cup sliced black olives
- Dollop each of salsa and sour cream

PREPARE PORK

In a medium-size bowl, add ketchup, brown sugar, apple cider vinegar and mesquite seasoning, and stir to combine. Divide the mixture in half. Place half in the refrigerator; set aside the other half.

In a slow cooker, add onion, apple and pork. Pour unrefrigerated half of mixture over pork. Cover and cook on high for 4 to 5 hours, or on low for 8 to 9 hours. (Note: Pork will be done when the bone pulls away from the meat.) Discard the bone and place pork on a cutting board, then shred the meat using two forks. (Note: If pork doesn't easily shred, it needs to be cooked longer.)

Strain the remaining liquid from the slow cooker; reserve ½ cup liquid and discard the rest. Make sure to also reserve onion and apple. Add onion and apple back to the slow cooker along with the shredded pork and reserved ½ cup liquid. Mix in the remaining ketchup mixture and heat for 15 to 20 more minutes.

To make into sandwiches: Keep on warm and serve with slaw and hamburger buns or potato rolls. For extra flavor, you can even add in your favorite barbecue sauce.

To make into nachos: Preheat oven or grill to 375°F.

Add chips to a foil-lined baking sheet. Cover chips with pulled pork and shredded cheese, then top with jalapeños. Bake or grill for 15 to 20 minutes, or until cheese is melted. Remove from heat and top with remaining ingredients.

MEATS
Salami
Capicola
Mortadella
Prosciutto
Sopressata

CHEESES
Brie
Parmesan
Goat
Smoked Gouda
Blue

ACCOMPANIMENTS
Olives
Pickled asparagus
Pepperoncini
Apricot preserves
Sundried tomatoes
Fresh fruit
Pesto (page 83)
Stone ground mustard
Crackers

BREADS
Baguette
Focaccia
Pretzel buns

NOTE

Feel free to add extra slices of meat and cheese to these sandwiches. I use items from the charcuterie platter along with some sliced turkey, ham and provolone.

Meat and cheese platters are always a good idea. I make one for every event that I host, whether big or small. For my boards, I like to add different breads, pestos and mustards so that my family and friends can make their perfect sandwich. This picnic image was taken at Sleeping Bear Dunes, a national park here in Michigan that *Good Morning America* named the "Most Beautiful Place in America" in 2011. Come check it out for yourself; it's awesome!

SERVES 4

CHARCUTERIE BOARD PICNIC

Arrange meats, cheeses and accompaniments on a large wooden cutting board. Serve with fruit, pesto, mustard, crackers and breads.

Make some focaccia and pretzel-bun sandwiches to serve alongside.

FOCACCIA SANDWICHES

Cut focaccia in half lengthwise.

Spread a thin layer of pesto over the cut sides of the bread. Layer meat on focaccia bottom, then add some cheese slices and top with some pepperoncini. Replace focaccia top and cut into desired slices. Arrange on a platter next to the charcuterie board.

PRETZEL-BUN SANDWICHES

Cut pretzel buns in half lengthwise.

Spread a thin layer of stone ground mustard over the cut sides of the buns. Layer meat on pretzel-bun bottom, followed by some cheese slices. Replace pretzel-bun top and cut into desired slices. Arrange on a platter next to the charcuterie board.

People in Michigan are serious about their Coney dogs. So, for you purists, remember that this is my take on the Coney dog. Yes, I use a pretzel bun and add pickled jalapeños (stop rolling your eyes). Don't knock it until you try it! If you want an authentic Coney dog, you must go to Detroit. We own RV resorts in Michigan, and one thing you can always count on at every site is people roasting hot dogs over a bonfire. Make these in your kitchen or over a campfire, or heat them in a muffler cooker while snowmobiling.

SERVES 8

CAMPFIRE CONEY DOGS

MAKE CONEY SAUCE

In a large nonstick skillet, add ground beef, garlic and 1 chopped onion, and cook over medium heat, about 6 minutes. Add tomato paste and thoroughly coat meat; cook for 1 to 2 more minutes. Add chili powder, paprika, salt, celery seeds, cumin, mustard, broth and brown sugar. Stir together until thoroughly combined. Reduce heat to medium-low and let simmer for 10 to 12 minutes.

PREPARE HOT DOGS

Place hot dogs in a saucepan and add enough water to cover them. Cover and cook on medium-high heat for 6 to 7 minutes, until heated all the way through. Slice hot dogs lengthwise down the center (but not all the way through). Split each hot dog open and place in a large skillet or on a grill for 1 to 2 minutes over medium-high heat to firm up the casings.

ASSEMBLE

Place each hot dog in a toasted bun, add some Coney Sauce and yellow mustard, then top with the remaining chopped onions. Add sliced jalapeños, if desired.

CONEY SAUCE

1 pound ground beef

2 cloves garlic, minced

2 small chopped onions, divided use

3 tablespoons tomato paste

2 teaspoons chili powder

1 teaspoon smoked paprika

1½ teaspoons salt

½ teaspoon celery seeds

1 teaspoon cumin

2 tablespoons yellow mustard, plus extra for topping

1 cup beef broth

2 tablespoons brown sugar

8 Koegel's Viennas (or favorite hot dog)

8 white or pretzel hot dog buns, split and lightly toasted

Pickled jalapeño slices, for garnish (optional)

Who doesn't like sloppy Joes? They are the easiest—and most economical—way to feed a crowd. I'm not a fan of mushy sloppy joes, so this recipe includes chips for crunch and French onion dip for a cool, creamy contrast to the ground beef. Perfect for game day!

SERVES 8 to 10

GAME DAY SLOPPY JOES

2 pounds ground beef

1 cup diced onion

1 cup diced bell pepper

2 cloves garlic, minced

1 (6-ounce) can tomato paste

¾ cup water

¼ cup brown sugar

1 tablespoon apple cider vinegar

1 tablespoon Dijon mustard

1 tablespoon Worcestershire sauce

1 tablespoon adobo sauce

1 teaspoon chili powder

1 tablespoon house seasoning

8 to 10 hamburger buns, split and lightly toasted

GARNISH

2 cups shredded cheddar cheese

1 (8-ounce) bag potato chips

1 cup French onion dip

PREPARE BEEF

In a large skillet over medium-high heat, add ground beef, onion, pepper and garlic, and cook until meat is no longer pink. Drain excess fat from skillet. Add the remaining ingredients to the ground beef mixture and simmer for 10 to 15 minutes.

ASSEMBLE

Add equal amounts of shredded cheese to each bun bottom, then top with some sloppy Joe mixture. Add some chips for a nice crunch, followed by a dollop of French onion dip. Cover with bun top.

TRAILGATING

We do a lot of snowmobiling in the winter on Michigan's 6,500-plus miles of groomed snowmobile trails. These meatballs are some of my favorite things to bring with us. I make these meatballs ahead of time, add them to my Muffpot (a special cooker that attaches to the snowmobile muffler), seal it up and off we go! Always cook the food fully first because the Muffpot will heat the food but not cook it from start to finish. People on the trails are amazed when we pull out these hot, juicy, gooey, cheesy meatballs for lunch on the snowy trails.

MAKES 18 MEATBALLS

MUFFLER MEATBALLS

- 1 cup breadcrumbs, or House-Seasoned Croutons (page 160)
- 1 cup heavy cream
- 1 pound ground beef
- 1 pound pork sausage
- 1 cup chopped onion
- 3 cloves garlic, minced
- 2 eggs, beaten
- ⅔ cup grated Parmesan, plus extra for topping
- ¼ cup chopped flat-leaf parsley
- 1 tablespoon House Seasoning (page 96)

Preheat oven to 425°F. Line a baking sheet with aluminum foil and spray with nonstick cooking spray.

In a small bowl, soak breadcrumbs or croutons in milk.

Crumble ground beef and sausage in a large mixing bowl. Add onion, garlic, eggs, Parmesan, parsley, House Seasoning and milk-soaked croutons. Gently mix together and form into round balls, roughly 2 ounces each (a little larger than a golf ball).

Place meatballs on foil-lined baking sheet and bake for 18 to 23 minutes, or until thoroughly cooked. Garnish with extra Parmesan. Refrigerate leftovers to use on your muffler cooker, Muffpot, when snowmobiling.

Make these ahead of time, and when you're ready to hit the trails with your snowmobile, line the muffler cooker with parchment paper. Add the cold meatballs and secure the cooker with the latches. Attach the cooker to the muffler and hit the trails. It takes 2 to 3 hours to heat the meatballs all the way through. Enjoy a hot meal on the trail.

NOTE

Heavy cream will add a creamy richness to these meatballs, but feel free to use milk for fewer calories.

I like to serve these in the Tomato Basil Soup recipe (page 193).

When people think of dips for game day tailgating, they usually think of something savory. But I love to take sweet dips as well. This is one that I have been making for years. When my daughter Ariana was at Michigan State University, we'd always go down and tailgate with her and her sorority sisters for Family Weekend or Homecoming. However, the dip always went missing before the party even started. I would bring several containers, and the girls would hide them in different refrigerators so they didn't have to share.

SERVES 4

SALTED CARAMEL
PEANUT BUTTER TOFFEE DIP

- ¼ cup toffee pieces
- 1 (8-ounce) package softened cream cheese
- 1 cup peanut butter
- 1 cup powdered sugar
- ¼ cup chocolate milk, chocolate cashew milk or espresso cold brew coffee
- ¼ cup caramel
- ⅛ teaspoon salt
- ⅛ teaspoon sea salt

GARNISH
Dark chocolate pretzels
Shortbread cookies

Grind toffee pieces in a food processor.

In a large bowl, add all remaining ingredients except the sea salt, and mix together to thoroughly combine. (Note: This can be done by hand or by using an electric mixer on medium speed.) Cover and refrigerate until ready to serve. When ready to serve, sprinkle dip with sea salt.

Serve with dark chocolate pretzels or shortbread cookies.

TRAILGATING

We're a big Jeeping family, and we love to take advantage of Michigan's 3,100-plus miles of off-roading trails, especially the ones in our backyard of Silver Lake. I bring food while we're out and heat it in foil under the hood on the car's manifold, which is how I became a *Jeep Talk Show* food and travel contributor. This bread bowl is by far my most requested recipe!

SERVES 4 to 6

SPINACH & ARTICHOKE
BACON BREAD BOWL

- 1 (22-ounce) bread bowl
- 1 (10-ounce) package frozen spinach, thawed
- 1 (14-ounce) can quartered artichoke hearts, drained and roughly chopped
- 1 (5-ounce) can water chestnuts, roughly chopped
- ¾ cup mayonnaise
- ¾ cup sour cream
- 2 cloves garlic, minced
- 1½ teaspoons House Seasoning (page 96)
- ½ cup grated Parmesan
- 1 cup shredded mozzarella or provolone cheese
- ¼ cup cooked and chopped bacon

Crackers

NOTE

Mix and match your favorite sandwiches using this technique. Try a pizza bread bowl, a lasagna bread bowl or a Reuben bread bowl.

PREPARE BREAD BOWL

Cut off the top of the bread bowl and hollow out most of the inside bread. Cube the inside bread and set aside.

PREPARE SPINACH

Place spinach in a clean towel and thoroughly wring out all liquid.

MAKE FILLING

In a large bowl, combine spinach, artichoke hearts, water chestnuts, mayonnaise, sour cream, garlic, House Seasoning, cheeses and bacon. Gently mix together all ingredients, then pour mixture into bread bowl.

Replace the bread bowl top and wrap the entire bowl in heavy-duty aluminum foil. (Use 1 layer of foil if heating in an oven. Use 2 to 3 layers if heating over a campfire or under the hood of your vehicle.)

BAKE BREAD BOWL

If using an oven, preheat oven to 375°F. Place foil-wrapped bread bowl in oven and bake for 40 to 45 minutes.

If using a grill or campfire, place foil-wrapped bread bowl over indirect heat. Heat for 20 to 30 minutes, or until cheeses are thoroughly melted.

If using the hood of your vehicle, place foil-wrapped bread bowl near a heat source under the hood. (Note: The best way to find this heat source is to drive the vehicle around to heat the engine, then turn off the vehicle.

Open the hood and feel for the best heat source. It usually is found near the exhaust manifold.) Make sure the bread bowl fits in a snug location so it doesn't move around. Also, make sure that the hood will compress the bread bowl but not squish it. This bread bowl is cheesy after 2 to 3 hours of being under the hood; be careful not to burn yourself when removing it.

If using your snowmobile or UTV, line 2 muffler cookers with parchment paper. Cut bread bowl in half and place one half in each muffler cooker. Latch the sides of the muffler cookers and attach to the exhaust. After 2 to 3 hours, you'll have a cheesy snack. Happy Trails!

ASSEMBLE

Unwrap the foil and serve spinach dip bowl with extra cubed bread and crackers.

Cooking in parchment is a great way to bake fish because it keeps the fish nice and moist without overcooking it. If I'm cooking in the oven, I use parchment paper, but if I am cooking on my grill or over a fire, then I use foil. My husband loves to fish. Me? Not so much. I remember the first time he took me fishing, I brought along a stack of magazines to read. He knew then and there that fishing wasn't my forté. But luckily for Ted, both of our daughters love to fish.

SERVES 4

STEELHEAD TROUT
IN PARCHMENT

- 1 pound fresh steelhead trout, cut into 4 equal-size fillets
- ½ teaspoon salt, divided use
- ¼ teaspoon pepper, divided use
- ¼ cup chili sauce (your favorite—Harissa (page 187), Sriracha, sweet chili sauce, sweet and spicy sauce)
- ¼ cup softened butter
- 3 cloves garlic, minced
- 1 pound baby potatoes, thinly sliced
- ½ pound broccoli florets
- 1 tablespoon canola oil

GARNISH

- Lemon
- Dill
- Cherry tomatoes

Preheat oven to 400°F. Lay out 4 pieces of parchment paper (at least 15 inches by 15 inches or larger). If using a grill or campfire, use aluminum foil.

Sprinkle trout with ¼ teaspoon of salt and ⅛ teaspoon of pepper.

In a small bowl, mix together chili sauce, butter, garlic and the remaining salt and pepper.

Place equal amounts of potatoes and broccoli on one half of each piece of parchment paper, then drizzle with oil. Place a fillet, skin-side down, over each set of potatoes and broccoli. Top each fillet with equal amounts of the butter mixture. Fold the parchment paper over and seal the edges, creating a half-moon shape. Place parchment packets on a rimmed baking sheet.

Bake for 15 to 18 minutes, or until potatoes and broccoli are cooked and fish is flaky.

Serve warm with fresh lemon, dill and cherry tomatoes.

Tater tots remind me of my childhood. Growing up, we'd always have fish sticks and tater tots with ketchup. I didn't like the fish sticks, so I'd trade my brothers for their tater tots. I always keep a bag of tater tots in the freezer, so if my family is craving cheeseburgers but I don't feel like grilling or forgot to buy buns, I make these. They are perfect hand-held treats for game day tailgating. Make these, and you'll never have leftovers after a party.

SERVES 18

DELUXE TATER TOT BITES

Preheat oven to 425°F. Spray an 18-cup regular-size muffin tin with nonstick cooking spray.

MAKE SPECIAL SAUCE

In a small bowl, add all ingredients and mix together until well-combined. Cover and refrigerate until ready to assemble.

PREPARE TATER TOTS

Place 5 tater tots inside each muffin cup, and bake for 20 minutes.

MAKE CHEESEBURGER FILLING

In a large skillet, add oil and onion, and cook over medium heat for 4 to 5 minutes. Add garlic and ground beef, and cook until meat is no longer pink. Stir in Worcestershire sauce, salt and pepper.

ASSEMBLE

Using the bottom of a shot glass or the back of an ice cream scooper, lightly press inside the center of each tater tot muffin cup to create a well. Spoon the meat mixture inside each tater tot well, then sprinkle cheese over meat. Bake for 5 more minutes.

Garnish with bacon bits, lettuce, tomatoes, pickles and special sauce.

SPECIAL SAUCE

½ cup mayonnaise

⅓ cup ketchup

1 tablespoon mustard

3 tablespoons dill relish

⅛ teaspoon sugar

⅛ teaspoon salt

⅛ teaspoon pepper

1 (2-pound) package tater tots

CHEESEBURGER FILLING

1 tablespoon canola oil

1 cup chopped onion

1 clove garlic, minced

1 pound lean ground beef

1 tablespoon Worcestershire sauce

1 teaspoon salt

1 teaspoon pepper

1 cup shredded cheddar cheese

GARNISH

Bacon bits

Shredded lettuce

Diced tomatoes

Dill relish or chopped dill pickles

I cook a lot of chili in the winter. It's the perfect comfort food. This recipe uses ground turkey, which is a great way to save a few calories. However, it also is great with ground beef, pork or even chicken. For game day tailgating, I make a large batch of this and keep it warm in the slow cooker, and then I set out tater tots or French fries (for chili cheese fries), corn bread, mini bags of Fritos and Doritos, and mini ciabatta loaves (for bread bowl chili).

SERVES 6 to 8

TURKEY CHILI

- 2 tablespoons olive oil
- ½ cup chopped sweet onion
- ½ cup chopped celery
- ½ cup chopped carrot
- 3 cloves garlic, minced
- 2 pounds ground turkey
- 1½ tablespoons chili powder
- 1 tablespoon ground cumin
- 1 tablespoon House Seasoning (page 96)
- 1½ tablespoons Dijon mustard
- 1 tablespoon honey
- 1 tablespoon tomato paste
- ½ cup red wine
- 1 cup dark red kidney beans
- 1 cup Great Northern beans
- 1 (15-ounce) can sweet corn, drained
- 1 cup chicken stock
- 1 (28-ounce) can diced tomatoes

GARNISH
Chopped celery leaves

OPTIONAL GARNISH
Shredded cheese
Sliced jalapeños
Sour cream
Black olives

MAKE CHILI

In a large saucepan or Dutch oven, add olive oil, onion, celery, carrot, garlic and ground turkey, and cook over medium-high heat for 8 to 10 minutes. Add chili powder, cumin and House Seasoning. Stir in Dijon mustard, honey and tomato paste. Cook for 1 to 2 minutes, then add red wine and cook for 3 to 4 more minutes. Stir in beans, corn, stock and diced tomatoes, then reduce the heat to medium and cook for 15 minutes.

ASSEMBLE

Add chili to bowls and garnish with celery leaves.

NOTE

Beans can be canned or dry. If using dry beans, soak beans overnight, then drain and use.

I like to serve this chili with a pat of butter on top of each bowl. For a game-day party, add chili to a slow cooker and keep on low.

Let me warn you: This is not a diet dip! People may think it's on the healthier side, since you use apple slices, but every delicious calorie of this dip is worth it. Make it in advance for tailgating parties or for a Thanksgiving app.

SERVES 4 to 6

APPLE FRITTER DIP

In a medium-size bowl, beat together butter, cream cheese and sugars until creamy. Add milk, corn syrup, vanilla, cinnamon, salt and apples, and mix thoroughly until well combined. Keep dip cold until ready to serve.

Slice top off apple fritter bread and set aside. Hollow out the soft inner bread and keep the crust as a shell. Cut the inside bread into bite-size pieces and set aside. These pieces will be used for dipping.

Add the dip to the inside of the apple fritter bread and garnish with diced apples.

Serve this dip with the leftover apple fritter bread pieces, apple slices, pretzels and/or doughnut holes.

1 stick butter, softened

1 (8-ounce) package cream cheese, softened

¼ cup brown sugar

½ cup confectioners' sugar

⅓ cup sweetened condensed milk

1 tablespoon light corn syrup

1 teaspoon vanilla extract

2 teaspoons ground cinnamon

⅛ teaspoon salt

2 honey crisp apples, finely diced, plus extra for garnish

1 loaf apple fritter bread

GARNISH

Apple slices

Pretzels

Chocolate-covered pretzels

Doughnut holes

6

FALL

If I had to pick a favorite season, I'd definitely pick fall. I love to pull out my cozy sweaters as the trees turn beautiful autumn colors. It's apple season and football season—time to root for our Detroit Lions. What more could a Michigan girl ask for? (Throw in watching my favorite Detroit Pistons and Red Wings at the new Little Caesars Arena, and I'm good!)

But there's so much more. We have ArtPrize, a huge international art festival in Grand Rapids. There are craft beer festivals, pumpkin patches and corn mazes, and it's a great time to visit Mackinac Island for its world-famous fudge.

Fall food to me is all about Thanksgiving. This is my favorite holiday to cook for, and I spend weeks shopping, prepping and enjoying every moment of it. I've even taken my deep fryer out in the snow to make my Jalapeño Onion Poppers to top the Green Bean Casserole (page 164).

LAKE OF THE CLOUDS
PORCUPINE MOUNTAINS

Luckily, in Michigan, we're surrounded by apples in fall. There are so many different varieties, all equally delicious. I personally don't love sweet potatoes, but I do love them loaded with apples, honey, butter and cinnamon—as they are in this recipe.

SERVES 4

APPLE CINNAMON LOADED SWEET POTATOES

- 4 medium sweet potatoes
- 2 Michigan apples (McIntosh, Jonathan or Honeycrisp), peeled, cored and diced
- ¼ cup chopped pecans
- 3 tablespoons sugar
- ½ teaspoon ground cinnamon
- ¼ cup Honey Cinnamon Sugar Butter (recipe below)

Preheat oven to 400°F.

PREPARE SWEET POTATOES

Pierce potatoes several times with a fork. Place potatoes on a baking sheet and bake for 45 minutes, or until fork-tender.

MAKE APPLE CINNAMON MIXTURE

While potatoes are baking, fold together apples, pecans, sugar and cinnamon in a medium bowl. Add apple mixture to a greased baking dish and bake for 30 minutes, or until apples are fork-tender. Set aside until ready to assemble.

ASSEMBLE

Make a slice in the top of each potato, lengthwise. Open the top and score the inside of each potato using a crosshatch pattern. Equally divide apple mixture into each potato. Top each potato with a dollop of Honey Cinnamon Sugar Butter. Serve warm.

HONEY CINNAMON SUGAR BUTTER

- ½ cup butter, softened
- 1½ tablespoons honey
- 1 teaspoon vanilla extract
- 3 teaspoons sugar
- ½ teaspoon ground cinnamon
- ⅛ teaspoon salt

Cream together all ingredients in a small bowl. Cover and refrigerate any unused butter.

I grew up always having—and loving!—chicken pot pie. It was a staple in our home. And there's something about the rich creaminess of spaghetti squash (my favorite squash) that makes the combination of these two foods just perfect. Add the flaky, crispy crust on top, and you're in fall heaven. Squash can be very hard to cut in half when it's raw, so my trick is to pierce it with a fork several times and then microwave it for about 5 minutes. It's easier to cut and also helps lessen the overall cooking time.

SERVES 4

CHICKEN POT PIE
SPAGHETTI SQUASH

Preheat oven to 400°F.

PREPARE SQUASH

Brush the inside of squash with canola oil, then place cut-side down on a baking dish. Bake for 30 to 40 minutes, or until fork-tender. Using a fork, lightly scrape the squash strands inside the shell. Sprinkle strands with salt and pepper, then set aside until ready to assemble.

MAKE POT PIE FILLING

While the squash is baking, make the pot pie filling. Add butter, sage and onion to a large skillet over medium heat and cook until onion is translucent, about 4 to 5 minutes. Stir in flour and cook for 1 to 2 more minutes. Add stock, salt and pepper, and continue to stir for 3 to 4 minutes. When mixture starts to thicken, add heavy cream. Turn heat down to low, then add veggies and chicken. Stir in Parmesan and remove from heat.

ASSEMBLE

Add ¾ cup pot pie filling to the inside of each squash half, and top with a piece of puff pastry. Brush pastry with egg and bake for 15 minutes, or until puff pastry is golden brown.

Garnish with fresh sage leaves.

SPAGHETTI SQUASH

2 medium spaghetti squash, halved and seeded

1 tablespoon canola oil

Salt and pepper

POT PIE FILLING

3 tablespoons butter

1 teaspoon chopped fresh sage

½ cup chopped onion

3 tablespoons flour

1½ cups chicken stock

¾ teaspoon salt

¼ teaspoon pepper

½ cup heavy cream

2 cups blanched mixed vegetables (peas, green beans, carrots, corn)

1 cup cooked chicken, cubed

¼ cup grated Parmesan cheese

1 sheet puff pastry, thawed and cut into 4 pieces the same size as spaghetti squash halves

1 egg, beaten

Fresh sage leaves, for garnish

NOTE

If fresh vegetables are not available or in season, use frozen mixed veggies that have been thawed.

This dish can be made without the spaghetti squash; simply add pot pie filling to ramekins and top with puff pastry (cut to individual size), then bake.

EGGPLANT PARMESAN
WITH SUN-DRIED TOMATO PESTO SAUCE

My daughter Ariana has always loved eggplant—even as a picky toddler! I remember when her friends came over, she'd convince them to eat it. Eggplant can be very bitter if you don't salt it first and get the water out. And, as with most things in life, eggplant is just meant to be deep-fried. I love being in the kitchen for hours and hours, but if that's not your thing, save time on this recipe by buying sun-dried tomato pesto sauce and marinara sauce instead of making them from scratch.

SERVES 4 to 6

2 medium eggplants, trimmed
Salt

DREDGE

1 cup flour
1 teaspoon House Seasoning (page 96)
3 eggs
½ cup water
1 cup Italian-style breadcrumbs

SAUCE

2 tablespoons olive oil
½ cup chopped onion
1 clove garlic, minced
1 (28-ounce) can crushed tomatoes
2 teaspoons sugar
1 teaspoon dried oregano
½ teaspoon salt
¼ teaspoon pepper
½ cup Sun-Dried Tomato Basil Pesto (recipe on facing page)

Canola oil, for frying

10 slices fresh mozzarella cheese (¼-inch thick)
½ cup shredded Parmesan cheese
Fresh basil, for garnish

NOTE

The sauce is good with or without the pesto.

Preheat oven to 400ºF.

PREPARE EGGPLANT

Cut each eggplant lengthwise into ¼-inch slices. Liberally salt both sides and set aside for 15 minutes.

PREPARE DREDGE

Set up dredging station with 3 shallow dishes (pie plates work great). Mix together flour and House Seasoning in the first dish. Beat eggs and water together in the second dish. Place breadcrumbs in the third dish.

DREDGE EGGPLANT

Blot each eggplant slice with paper towel to remove excess salt and moisture. Dredge each slice first in the flour, then the egg wash, then the breadcrumbs. Set aside until ready to fry.

PREPARE SAUCE

In a large saucepan, add oil and onion, and cook over medium heat for 4 to 5 minutes. Turn heat to medium-low and add garlic. Cook for 1 minute, then add tomatoes, sugar, oregano, salt, pepper and pesto. Cook for 10 to 12 minutes, stirring occasionally. Taste and add extra seasonings or sugar, as necessary. Set aside until ready to assemble.

FRY EGGPLANT

Add canola oil to a deep, heavy pot. Heat oil over medium heat. Fry each eggplant slice for 3 to 5 minutes on each side, or until golden brown. Remove and drain on a paper towel. (Fry in batches; don't crowd the pot.)

ASSEMBLE

Add ½ cup of sauce to the bottom of a 9-by-13-inch baking dish. Layer eggplant slices in dish, then top with mozzarella cheese and more sauce. Sprinkle shredded Parmesan over top and bake for 20 to 25 minutes, or until cheese is melted and bubbly. Garnish with fresh basil and serve warm.

SUN-DRIED TOMATO BASIL PESTO

1 cup fresh basil leaves

¼ cup sun-dried tomatoes packed in oil

2 tablespoons tomato paste

2 cloves garlic

½ cup grated Parmesan cheese

½ cup olive oil

¼ teaspoon salt

¼ teaspoon pepper

¼ teaspoon sugar

Add all ingredients to a food processor and process for 2 to 3 minutes, scraping down the sides as necessary. Store in refrigerator until ready to use.

SERVES 6 to 8

FALL HARVEST SALAD

This is my basic salad that I always make and then alter based on the season. I keep the mixed greens and dressing the same, but during the fall, I add roasted vegetables like sweet potatoes and kohlrabi. This is my sister's favorite. She always begs me to make it when we visit her in Marco Island, Florida. Be sure to make tons of this dressing, as it goes well with so many things.

ROASTED VEGGIES

- 1 cup peeled and cubed kohlrabi
- 1 cup peeled and cubed beets
- 1 cup peeled and cubed sweet potato
- 3 tablespoons Zoye Premium Vegetable Oil®
- 1½ tablespoons House Seasoning (page 96)

SESAME GINGER DRESSING

- ¼ cup rice wine vinegar
- 2 tablespoons soy sauce
- ½ teaspoon sugar
- 1 teaspoon minced garlic
- 1 teaspoon minced ginger
- ¼ teaspoon red-pepper flakes
- ½ teaspoon toasted sesame oil
- ¼ cup Zoye Premium Vegetable Oil®

- 2 cups chopped kale
- 2 cups mixed greens
- 1 cup cooked quinoa
- ¼ cup feta cheese crumbles
- Roasted Pepitas (recipe below)

ROASTED PEPITAS

- ¼ cup raw pumpkin seeds (pepitas)
- 2 teaspoons Zoye Premium Vegetable Oil®
- ⅛ teaspoon salt
- ⅛ teaspoon ground ginger

Preheat oven to 350°F.

Mix seeds, oil and seasonings together. Place seasoned seeds on a baking sheet and roast for 12 to 15 minutes.

Preheat oven to 400°F.

PREPARE VEGGIES

Add 3 sheets of aluminum foil to a baking sheet. Add kohlrabi, beets and sweet potato to each piece of foil. Season with oil and House Seasoning, then roast for 15 to 20 minutes, or until fork-tender. Remove from the oven and set aside. (I like to keep the veggies separate while roasting; otherwise, the beets will turn the rest pink.)

MAKE DRESSING

In a small bowl, mix together vinegar, soy sauce, sugar, garlic, ginger and red-pepper flakes. Drizzle in oils and whisk to emulsify the dressing. Set aside until ready to assemble.

Add 2 tablespoons of dressing to kale, and massage well to soften kale.

ASSEMBLE

Add kale and mixed greens to a large salad dish. Add the roasted kohlrabi, beets and sweet potato, then top with quinoa. Drizzle on some dressing and sprinkle with feta cheese crumbles. Add Roasted Pepitas, if desired.

NOTE

I cook my quinoa in chicken broth along with some ground cumin and salt. This is a great way to impart flavor into the quinoa.

This is the most beautiful salad. Your guests will be so impressed with the vibrant color of the radishes and the crazy shape of the Romanesco. And it's deliciously balanced, too! If you need a salad to pass around at a party or gathering, use the radish as a little taco shell and place the ingredients inside. Then use a mini-clip or something cute to hold each taco together. It's a dish your friends will always remember.

SERVES 4

WATERMELON RADISH AND ROMANESCO SALMON SALAD

PREPARE SALMON

Place salmon fillets and ¼ cup of vinaigrette in a resealable plastic bag, and marinate in the refrigerator for at least 30 minutes, or up to 2 hours.

Discard marinade and pat fillets dry. Season both sides with salt and pepper. Heat canola oil in a large nonstick skillet over medium heat. Place fillets in skillet, skin-side down, and cook for 3 to 4 minutes. Flip and cook for 3 to 4 more minutes.

PREPARE ROMANESCO

Remove leaves from broccoli and break off florets. Add florets and salt to 2 inches of water in a medium saucepan, and bring to a boil. Turn off the heat, cover and let steam for 10 minutes.

ASSEMBLE

Place arugula and spring mix on a large serving platter. Add salmon fillets whole or lightly flaked over the greens. Add florets and crumbled goat cheese. Top with watermelon radish slices, and drizzle entire dish with the remaining vinaigrette. Garnish with fresh dill fronds.

I like to add this salad and salmon to the inside of thinly sliced watermelon radishes for a low-carb taco option. Watermelon radishes make a great mini taco shell, and they are perfect as a hand-held party food for events.

SALMON

4 (6-ounce) salmon fillets, skin on

½ cup Honey Dijon Red Wine Vinaigrette (page 52), divided use

½ teaspoon salt

¼ teaspoon pepper

1 tablespoon canola oil

ROMANESCO

1 head Romanesco broccoli

¼ teaspoon salt

2 cups arugula

4 cups spring mix

2 ounces crumbled goat cheese

1 watermelon radish, thinly sliced

GARNISH

Fresh dill fronds

NOTE

Feel free to substitute goat cheese with Havarti dill cheese.

Prepare watermelon radish just like a regular radish: simply wash and cut off the ends, then thinly slice.

When Romanesco broccoli is not in season, substitute with cauliflower or broccoli.

When watermelon radishes aren't in season, substitute with red radishes.

SQUASH

- 1 butternut squash, cut in half lengthwise and seeded
- 2 tablespoons melted butter
- Pinch of salt and pepper
- 2 tablespoons brown sugar

BALSAMIC REDUCTION

- ¾ cup balsamic vinegar
- 3 tablespoons brown sugar

MAPLE DIJON VINAIGRETTE

- 3 tablespoons maple syrup
- 3 tablespoons Dijon mustard
- ½ cup olive oil
- ¼ cup rice wine vinegar
- 1 clove garlic, minced
- ½ shallot, minced
- ½ teaspoon salt
- ¼ teaspoon pepper

HAYSTACKS

- ½ cup butterscotch morsels
- ¼ cup peanut butter
- 1 cup chow mein noodles

SALAD

- 1 cup mixed greens
- ½ cup cherry tomatoes, halved
- 1 cup cooked red quinoa

NOTE

I cook the quinoa with vegetable or chicken broth, and add some salt, cumin, granulated garlic and nutmeg to the broth before it is absorbed to add some flavor.

Forget the side dishes; this is an entire meal in one—protein, greens and grains. It's great for a meatless Monday or to serve at Thanksgiving for your vegetarian friends. I love the sweet crunch on top and the beautiful presentation.

SERVES 2

HAYSTACK SQUASH SALAD
BUTTERNUT BROWN SUGAR QUINOA BOWL

PREPARE SQUASH

Preheat oven to 400°F.

Place butternut squash halves on a baking sheet, flesh-side up. Brush melted butter over squash flesh, then sprinkle with salt, pepper and brown sugar. Bake for 45 to 55 minutes, or until fork-tender.

Scoop out some of the butternut squash flesh (approximately 1 to 2 tablespoons from each half) to make a well from top to bottom, and set aside. Mash the scooped-out squash with a fork and set aside. Cross-hatch the remainder of the squash halves.

MAKE REDUCTION

In a small saucepan, add balsamic vinegar and brown sugar. Bring to a boil, then reduce heat to simmer. Cook until the balsamic mixture is reduced by half. Set aside.

MAKE VINAIGRETTE

Whisk together all ingredients and refrigerate until ready to assemble.

MAKE HAYSTACKS

In a small bowl, add butterscotch morsels and microwave for 30 seconds at a time until softened. Add peanut butter and stir until thoroughly combined. Add chow mein noodles to mixture and gently fold together. Drop by spoonfuls onto wax paper until cooled.

ASSEMBLE

Evenly distribute mixed greens and tomatoes in each squash half. Top with quinoa and remaining mashed squash, then drizzle with vinaigrette followed by balsamic reduction. Add haystacks to the tops and serve.

I don't know why every poultry dish is not made this way. Whether I'm making roast chicken, turkey or Cornish hen, I stuff the caps of mushrooms with butter. As the bird roasts, the mushrooms act as little moisture emitters—they keep the meat so juicy! Don't worry if you don't like mushrooms; this dish does not taste like them.

SERVES 4

GARLICKY MUSHROOM STUFFED ROAST CHICKEN

GARLICKLY MUSHROOMS

16 ounces whole button mushrooms, stemmed

½ cup Garlic-Herb Compound Butter (recipe below)

CHICKEN

1 (3- to 4-pound) roaster chicken

2 tablespoons Garlic-Herb Compound Butter

2 tablespoons canola oil

1 tablespoon House Seasoning (page 96)

1 large onion, peeled and sliced

¼ cup chicken stock

Fresh parsley or chives

Fresh sage and thyme

GARLIC-HERB COMPOUND BUTTER

1 cup butter, softened

1 clove garlic, minced

1 tablespoon fresh sage, roughly chopped

1 tablespoon fresh thyme, roughly chopped

Mix together butter, garlic and herbs in a small bowl.

Preheat oven to 400° F.

PREPARE MUSHROOMS

Clean mushrooms with a damp paper towel. Place about 1 tablespoon of garlic-herb butter into each mushroom cap. Set aside.

PREPARE CHICKEN

Remove giblets from chicken cavity and discard. Dry the skin of the chicken with a paper towel. Rub butter all over chicken and under the skin of the breasts. (Be careful not to break the skin.) Rub oil over the buttered skin and sprinkle with House Seasoning. Place half of the mushrooms inside the chicken cavity, then tie the legs together with twine. Tuck the wings under, then place the remaining mushrooms in the center of a roasting pan, butter-side up. Place chicken on top of mushrooms, then add onion to roasting pan. Pour chicken stock over onion.

ROAST CHICKEN

Roast chicken for approximately 1½ hours, or until thermometer reaches 165°F. (After 30 minutes, I place a piece of aluminum foil over the chicken so it doesn't brown too much. Don't wrap foil around chicken; lightly tent it over the top.)

When chicken is thoroughly cooked, remove mushrooms from cavity and place in the hot pan drippings. Lightly tent chicken with foil and let sit for at least 20 minutes before carving. Remove onion from drippings and place in a serving dish; keep warm until ready to eat.

ASSEMBLE

Add mushrooms to a separate serving dish, and keep warm. Sprinkle with fresh parsley or chives.

Serve chicken with fresh sage and thyme, onion, mushrooms and gravy. Complete this meal with the Dried Cranberry Sage Stuffing (page 160).

GRAVY

Pan drippings (approximately 1 cup)

1 cup chicken stock

2 tablespoons cornstarch

Salt and pepper

Strain pan drippings into a measuring cup and let rest until the fat separates. Skim off any fat from pan drippings and discard. Add rest of drippings to a saucepan over medium heat. In a small bowl, whisk together chicken stock and cornstarch. Slowly pour mixture into hot drippings to make the gravy. Whisk until thoroughly combined and thickened. Season to taste.

NOTE

I stuff both chickens and turkeys this way, with garlic-herb-buttered mushrooms. The mushrooms help moisten the meat while roasting, and the mushrooms are perfectly browned, roasted and seasoned when done.

If you forget to lightly tent the chicken with foil and the skin starts to burn, flip the chicken over, breast-side down, into the juices; this will help prevent the chicken from drying out.

If you're roasting a turkey, add all mushrooms to the cavity and place the turkey on a roasting rack inside a roasting pan. Roast at 325°F for 15 minutes per pound, or until fully cooked.

One of my favorite things to do is make stuffing. I guess this recipe technically should be called "dressing" because I never stuff it in the bird. But I grew up calling it "stuffing"! Everyone loves cranberries for the holidays, so add some dried cranberries for extra texture and flavor. Take the additional time to make your own croutons—it makes all the difference in this dish.

SERVES 6 to 8

DRIED CRANBERRY SAGE STUFFING

DAIRY FREE

HOUSE-SEASONED CROUTONS

- ½ cup olive oil
- 2 cloves garlic, grated
- 1 tablespoon House Seasoning (page 96)
- 1 pound French baguette or country bread, cubed (about 8 to 10 cups)

STUFFING

- 16 ounces sage pork sausage
- 1 cup chopped onions
- 1 cup chopped celery
- 8 ounces chopped button or cremini mushrooms
- 1 teaspoon chopped sage
- 1 teaspoon chopped thyme
- 6 to 8 cups house-seasoned croutons (see recipe above)
- ½ cup dried cranberries
- 2 to 3 cups chicken stock

Preheat oven to 400°F.

PREPARE CROUTONS

Combine olive oil, garlic and House Seasoning. Add the cubed bread to a bowl, then toss in the oil mixture to thoroughly combine. Add bread to 2 large baking sheets. Bake for 12 to 15 minutes. Set aside until ready to assemble. Turn oven down to 350°F.

PREPARE SAUSAGE

Cook sausage in a skillet over medium heat for 8 to 10 minutes, or until thoroughly cooked. With a slotted spoon, remove sausage and place on a paper towel to drain.

PREPARE ONIONS, CELERY AND MUSHROOMS

Add onions, celery and mushrooms to reserved sausage drippings in skillet and cook for 4 to 5 minutes. Add sage and thyme, and cook for 1 to 2 more minutes.

ASSEMBLE

In a large bowl, add croutons, onion-celery-mushroom mixture, sausage and dried cranberries. Slowly add chicken stock, ½ cup at a time. (I usually use about 2½ cups of stock.) Continue to gently fold everything together until croutons are moist, but not too wet. Add stuffing to a greased 9-by-13-inch baking dish and bake for 30 to 40 minutes, uncovered.

NOTE

We always call this "stuffing," even though we don't stuff it inside chicken or turkey. So, technically, it's "dressing" and not "stuffing." But use it any way you see fit.

GG is for "Ginger and Garlic," but it's also the name my granddaughter gave me. This dish combines two of my favorite ingredients in the world: Brussels sprouts and soy sauce. I'll eat Brussels sprouts any way, but this dish is just so balanced with the freshness of the lemon, the punch of the ginger and saltiness of the soy sauce. Be sure to use both the ground ginger and fresh ginger paste to get the full flavor profile.

SERVES 4

GG'S BRUSSELS SPROUTS

- 1 pound Brussels sprouts, cleaned and halved
- 1 teaspoon toasted sesame oil
- 1 teaspoon garlic paste
- ¼ teaspoon granulated garlic
- 1 teaspoon ginger paste
- ¼ teaspoon ground ginger
- ¼ teaspoon salt
- ⅛ teaspoon black pepper
- ½ teaspoon red-pepper flakes
- 6 slices thick-cut bacon, chopped
- 1 tablespoon soy sauce
- Juice of ½ lemon

Preheat oven to 400°F.

ROAST BRUSSELS SPROUTS

Toss Brussels sprouts with sesame oil, garlic paste, garlic, ginger paste, ginger, salt, pepper and red-pepper flakes. Place on a parchment paper-lined baking sheet and roast for 15 to 18 minutes.

PREPARE BACON

While the Brussels sprouts are roasting, add bacon to a skillet and cook over medium heat for 8 to 10 minutes. Remove bacon with a slotted spoon and place on a paper towel to drain.

ASSEMBLE

Toss Brussels sprouts and bacon together. Pour soy sauce and fresh lemon juice over entire dish. Serve warm.

The key to this dish is to use fresh green beans and homemade cream of mushroom soup. Don't buy it in a can! You can make the components of this dish a few days in advance to ease the holiday chaos. Instead of using fried onion strings on top, I make enough jalapeño poppers for the amount of people I have coming to dinner, so everyone gets at least one. I don't like to fry food inside, so I take my little FryDaddy outside—even in the snow!

SERVES 8 to 10

GREEN BEAN CASSEROLE
TOPPED WITH JALAPEÑO ONION POPPERS

- 3 pounds fresh green beans, trimmed
- 3 tablespoons butter
- ½ cup chopped onion
- 8 ounces chopped button mushrooms
- 1 clove garlic, minced
- 3 tablespoons flour
- 2 ounces cooking sherry (optional)
- 1 cup chicken stock
- 1 cup heavy cream
- 1¼ teaspoons House Seasoning (page 96)
- ½ cup grated Parmesan cheese

Preheat oven to 350°F.

PREPARE GREEN BEANS

Fill a large stock pot ⅔ full with salted water and bring to a boil. Add green beans and blanch for 4 to 5 minutes, then plunge beans into an ice bath to stop the cooking process. Drain and set aside.

MAKE SAUCE

Add butter, onion, mushrooms and garlic to a large skillet over medium heat and cook for 5 minutes, or until mushroom liquid starts to reabsorb. Add flour and cook for 1 to 2 more minutes. Add sherry and cook for 1 minute, stirring constantly. Stir in chicken stock and heavy cream. Cook until it starts to thicken, then add House Seasoning and Parmesan. Once everything starts to bubble, continue to stir and cook for another 4 to 5 minutes.

BAKE CASSEROLE

Add green beans to sauce and stir until everything is well-incorporated. Add the mixture to a greased 2-quart baking dish and bake for 15 to 20 minutes, or until bubbly.

PREPARE JALAPEÑO ONION POPPERS

In a small bowl, mix together cream cheese, shredded cheese and jalapeños. Spread equal portions of the cream cheese mixture to the inside of each onion slice, then freeze for 10 minutes or until firm.

PREPARE DREDGE

Set up dredging station with 3 shallow dishes (pie plates work great). Mix flour and ½ teaspoon of salt in the first dish. Beat together egg and milk in the second dish. Place breadcrumbs in the third dish. One at a time, dredge the onion slices first in the flour mixture, then in the egg mixture, then in the breadcrumbs.

FRY ONION POPPERS

Heat oil in a deep, heavy pot over medium heat. Carefully add onion slices to the hot oil, making sure they do not clump together. Fry for 3 to 4 minutes, turning as needed until crisp and golden-brown. Drain on paper towels. Sprinkle remaining ½ teaspoon of salt over onion poppers while hot.

ASSEMBLE

Top green bean casserole with Jalapeño Onion Poppers (recipe at right) and serve warm.

JALAPEÑO ONION POPPERS

SERVES 8 TO 10

Peanut or canola oil, for frying

4 ounces cream cheese

3 tablespoons shredded cheddar cheese

1 tablespoon chopped jalapeños

1 sweet onion, peeled and cut into ½-inch-thick slices

¼ teaspoon House Seasoning (page 96)

DREDGE

½ cup flour

1 teaspoon kosher salt, divided use

2 eggs

½ cup milk

1 cup panko breadcrumbs, divided use

FROSTED FLAKES APPLE CRISP

SERVES 8

TOPPING

- 1 cup flour
- 1/8 teaspoon salt
- 1/4 teaspoon ground cinnamon
- 1/2 cup brown sugar
- 1/2 cup butter
- 1 cup Kellogg's Frosted Flakes®

APPLE CRISP

- 8 Michigan apples (Northern Spy, Cortland and/or Gala), peeled and cubed
- Juice of 1 lemon
- 2/3 cup sugar
- 1 teaspoon ground cinnamon
- 1/8 teaspoon ground ginger
- 1/8 teaspoon salt

CRUST

- 2 cups finely ground graham crackers (approximately 2 sleeves)
- 3 tablespoons sugar
- 1/2 cup butter, melted
- 1/8 teaspoon salt

ICE CREAM PIE

- 1 1/2 quarts vanilla ice cream
- 1 1/2 cups Frosted Flakes® Apple Crisp (recipe above)

TOPPING

- 1/2 cup Kellogg's Frosted Flakes®
- 1/4 cup caramel sauce
- 1/2 teaspoon flake sea salt

For me, this dish is synonymous with fall. Growing up, there was a restaurant that made apple pie ice cream once a year. I looked forward to going there with my grandparents every fall. I always thought, "When I grow up, I'm learning how to make this!" In my recipe, make the apple crisp first, then when you have leftovers, you can make the apple crisp ice cream pie.

SERVES 8

APPLE CRISP ICE CREAM PIE
TOPPED WITH SALTED CARAMEL FROSTED FLAKES

Preheat oven to 350°F.

FOR APPLE CRISP:

PREPARE TOPPING

Mix together flour, salt, cinnamon and brown sugar in a medium-size bowl. Cut in butter with a pastry cutter or your fingers until crumbly. Add Frosted Flakes and mix to thoroughly combine. Set aside.

PREPARE CRISP

Place apples in a 2-quart baking dish, then add lemon juice. Sprinkle sugar, cinnamon, ginger and salt over apples, and mix to thoroughly combine.

BAKE

Add topping and bake for 50 to 55 minutes and enjoy.

FOR APPLE CRISP ICE CREAM PIE:

PREPARE CRUST

Mix together crust ingredients and press into a greased pie dish. Refrigerate crust for at least 1 hour.

ASSEMBLE

Combine ice cream and leftover Apple Crisp together in a large bowl, then add to the chilled pie crust. Cover and freeze overnight.

SERVE

Top pie with cereal, caramel sauce and sea salt. Cut into 8 slices and serve cold. Freeze any leftovers.

> **NOTE**
>
> Mix and match whatever graham crackers you would like—regular, honey or chocolate. The photo here is one package chocolate and one package honey.

You'll never get me to eat a piece of pumpkin pie, but I'll devour these bars. The coconut flavor and icing are just out of this world. I always keep them cold in the fridge. If you don't have coconut flour, you can substitute all-purpose, but it obviously will change the flavor and texture.

SERVES 12

PECAN PUMPKIN BARS
WITH MAPLE CREAM CHEESE FROSTING

Preheat oven to 325°F. Spray a 9-by-13-inch baking dish with nonstick cooking spray.

MAKE PUMPKIN BARS

In a medium bowl, sift together flours, baking powder, baking soda, cinnamon and salt. Set aside.

Using an electric stand mixer with a paddle attachment, cream together eggs, sugar, oil and pumpkin on medium-high speed for 2 to 3 minutes. Turn the mixer to low and slowly add the dry ingredients; beat until thoroughly combined, scraping down the side of the bowl as necessary. Fold in the pecans and continue to mix until all ingredients are well-incorporated.

Pour the pumpkin mixture into baking dish, and spread out evenly. Bake for 30 to 40 minutes, or until a toothpick inserted into the center comes clean.

MAKE FROSTING

Combine all frosting ingredients, and beat together until creamy.

ASSEMBLE

Frost the bars when cooled, then cut into squares. Top with extra chopped nuts.

PUMPKIN BARS

1 cup four
¾ cup coconut flour
½ teaspoon baking powder
¼ teaspoon baking soda
1 teaspoon ground cinnamon
⅛ teaspoon salt
4 eggs
1¾ cups sugar
¾ cup canola oil
1 (15-ounce) can 100-percent pure pumpkin
¼ cup chopped pecans, plus extra for garnish

FROSTING

8 ounces cream cheese, softened
1 cup powdered sugar
½ cup butter, softened
¼ cup maple syrup
1 teaspoon vanilla extract
¼ teaspoon pumpkin pie spice
⅛ teaspoon salt

When people hear that **I'm putting squash** in a dessert, they're initially a little weirded out. But what most people don't realize is that most cans of pumpkin—you know, the cans that you make pumpkin pie with every year—are actually a variety of squashes. Don't believe me? Check the ingredients label! I'm here to debunk the myth that squash and pumpkin don't have similar tastes. Try this recipe, and you'll be a squash-dessert believer.

SERVES 12

SCOTCHIE SQUASH CHEESECAKE BARS

SQUASH

- 1 cup peeled and diced butternut squash (similar in size to butterscotch morsels used in recipe)
- 1 teaspoon vegetable oil
- ⅛ teaspoon salt
- ¼ teaspoon sugar
- ¼ teaspoon pumpkin-pie spice

CRUST

- 2 cups chocolate graham crackers or Oreo cookies, finely ground in a food processor
- ¾ cup melted butter
- 3 tablespoons sugar

CHEESECAKE LAYER

- 2 (8-ounce) packages cream cheese, softened
- 1 cup sugar
- ½ cup sour cream
- 3 eggs
- 1 cup flour
- ⅛ teaspoon salt
- 1 teaspoon artificial butter flavoring
- 1 teaspoon vanilla extract

Preheat oven to 375°F. Spray a 9-by-13-inch pan with nonstick cooking spray.

ROAST SQUASH

In a small bowl, toss together squash, oil, salt, sugar and pumpkin-pie spice. Add squash to a rimmed baking sheet and roast for 10 minutes. Remove from heat and set aside. Reduce heat to 325°F.

PREPARE CRUST

Mix ground graham crackers, melted butter and sugar in a bowl. Press the graham cracker mixture into the bottom of the prepared pan.

PREPARE CHEESECAKE LAYER

In a large bowl, cream together the cream cheese and sugar. Add sour cream, eggs, flour, salt, butter flavoring and vanilla. Continue mixing together until well-incorporated. Pour the cheesecake mixture over the graham cracker crust.

PREPARE OATMEAL COOKIE LAYER

In a large bowl, cream together the butter and sugars until thoroughly combined. Add eggs and vanilla. Add flour, baking soda, salt and cinnamon until well-combined, then gently add oats and butterscotch morsels. Fold in the roasted butternut squash, then dollop this mixture on top of the cream cheese layer.

OATMEAL COOKIE LAYER

- 1 cup butter, softened
- 1 cup brown sugar
- ½ cup sugar
- 2 eggs
- 1 teaspoon vanilla extract
- 1¼ cups flour, sifted
- ½ teaspoon baking soda
- ½ teaspoon salt
- ½ teaspoon ground cinnamon
- 2 cups oats
- 1 cup butterscotch morsels, plus extra for topping

Hot fudge, chocolate sauce, caramel sauce and/or butterscotch sauce, for garnish (optional)

NOTE

The easiest way to peel a butternut squash is to cut off the ends, pierce it several times with a fork and microwave for 5 minutes. Let cool, then halve, peel, seed and dice.

ASSEMBLE

Bake at 325°F for 50 to 60 minutes, or until a toothpick inserted into the center comes clean. Cover and refrigerate overnight (or at least 3 hours), then cut into bars. Drizzle with hot fudge, chocolate sauce, caramel sauce and/or butterscotch topping, if desired, then serve.

SILVER LAKE SAND DUNES

7

WINTER

Michigan is truly a winter wonderland, and we try to take full advantage of it. As kids, we would ride snowmobiles through the fields and orchards from our grandparents' farm to our friends' house down the way. No roads—just pure backwoods snow. It was like something out of a movie. Our love of snowmobiling is even stronger today, now that we have kids of our own. Our big family snowmobiling escapades always end with a big pan of Cheesy Enchiladas (page 177) or Tomato Basil Soup (page 193). Also, an advantage of growing up near a ski resort was that Monday nights were huge—not because of football, but because it was Ski Club Night at our school. It was so much fun!

Chances are, no matter where you live in the U.S., you have had a Michigan Christmas tree. Michigan is known for having some of the best Christmas trees in the world. We're actually third in the nation for harvesting them. Every year, we go out into the snow-covered forests, cut one down and bring it back, Griswold-style. And as we are decorating the tree, we always have a big pot of Pappardelle Pepper-Crusted Beef Ragu (page 190) simmering away.

Whether it's Thanksgiving, Christmas, Easter—you name the holiday—I'm making this casserole. It's a crowd-pleaser, and it's so simple because you can (read: "should") make it the night before and pop it in the oven the next morning. Depending on how much company we are hosting, I usually make two casseroles: one with different meats like ham, bacon or sausage, and another that's just veggies. The Pinconning cheese is a great Michigan touch. It's kind of like an aged Colby and is great in casseroles and mac and cheese.

SERVES 12

HOLIDAY BREAKFAST CASSEROLE

- 16 ounces pork sausage
- ⅛ teaspoon red-pepper flakes
- ¼ cup BLiS Bourbon Barrel-Aged Maple Syrup

- 10 eggs
- 2 cups milk
- 1 teaspoon salt
- ¼ teaspoon pepper
- 3 cups House-Seasoned Croutons (page 160), or store bought
- 2 cups shredded Pinconning or Colby cheese

NOTE

Feel free to substitute regular maple syrup for bourbon barrel-aged maple syrup.

Preheat oven to 350°F. Spray a 9-by-13-inch baking dish with nonstick cooking spray.

PREPARE SAUSAGE

Cook sausage in a skillet over medium-high heat, for 8 to 10 minutes, or until no longer pink. Add red-pepper flakes and maple syrup.

ASSEMBLE

In a large bowl, whisk together eggs, milk, salt and pepper.

Place croutons in the bottom of the baking dish. Crumble sausage and sprinkle evenly over croutons, then pour egg mixture over sausage. Press down and make sure everything is thoroughly coated with egg mixture. (If making this the night before, cover and refrigerate.) Evenly sprinkle cheese over entire dish.

Bake for 45 to 55 minutes, or until eggs are cooked.

I love to make enchiladas whenever I have leftover chicken, turkey or beef. They're always a great way to get your kids to eat corn and beans. For some reason, they eat anything wrapped in a tortilla. Feel free to use rotisserie chicken to save a step, but make the enchilada sauce yourself. It makes all the difference and is so simple, since it uses ingredients you probably already have on hand.

SERVES 4 to 6

CHEESY ENCHILADAS

Preheat oven to 350°F. Spray a 9-by-13-inch baking dish with nonstick cooking spray.

MAKE SAUCE

In a medium saucepan, heat oil or butter and flour over medium heat, and stir to combine. Cook for 1 to 2 minutes to cook out the flour taste. Add chicken stock and tomato paste. Whisk together, then add chili powder, cumin and House Seasoning. Cook for 6 to 8 minutes, or until sauce is thickened. Reduce heat to simmer and keep warm until ready to assemble.

MAKE ENCHILADAS

Mix together meat, sour cream, half of the cheese, corn and black beans in a large bowl.

Microwave all tortillas for 20 to 30 seconds to soften.

ASSEMBLE

Spread ½ cup of enchilada sauce over the bottom of the baking dish. Spoon an equal amount of meat mixture down the center of each tortilla. Roll up and place each tortilla, seam-side down, next to each other in the baking dish. Pour enchilada sauce over tortillas, then sprinkle with remaining cheese.

Bake for 30 minutes, or until bubbly. Top with avocado, tomatoes, black olives and cilantro.

ENCHILADA SAUCE

- 2 tablespoons canola oil or butter
- 2 tablespoons flour
- 2 cups chicken stock
- 3 tablespoons tomato paste
- 2 teaspoons chili powder
- 1 teaspoon cumin
- 3 teaspoons House Seasoning (page 96)

- 2 cups cooked and shredded chicken or turkey
- ⅔ cup sour cream
- 2 cups shredded cheddar cheese, divided use
- 1 (15-ounce) can sweet corn, drained
- 1 (15-ounce) can black beans, drained
- 10 corn tortillas

GARNISH

- Diced avocado
- Tomatoes
- Sliced black olives
- Cilantro

NOTE

Add ½ cup of homemade Harissa (page 187) to enchilada sauce to add additional spice to this recipe.

SAUCE

- 1 head garlic
- 1 tablespoon olive oil, divided
- 1 sweet onion, halved, peeled and thinly sliced
- 1 (28-ounce) can crushed tomatoes
- ¼ cup fresh basil
- ½ teaspoon salt
- 1 teaspoon oregano
- 1 teaspoon granulated garlic
- 1½ tablespoons sugar

CRUST

- 2⅓ cups bread flour, plus more for dusting
- 2 teaspoons salt
- 1 teaspoon instant yeast
- ½ teaspoon sugar
- 1 cup warm water (95-105°F)
- Oil, for greasing bowl

- Butter and oil, for greasing pans
- 32 to 40 pepperoni slices
- 1½ cups freshly shredded brick cheese
- 1½ cups freshly shredded mozzarella cheese
- Fresh basil, for garnish

NOTE

Another option is to split the dough in half and use two 8-by-10-inch Detroit-style steel pans. Bake for 15 to 18 minutes.

Brick cheese, which is authentic for Detroit-style pizza, can be hard to find. Feel free to substitute it with sharp white cheddar.

Add extra sugar and/or seasonings to the pizza sauce, depending on the sweetness of the tomatoes.

My favorite pizza is Detroit-style pizza. Authentic Detroit-style crust is thick and has a light and airy inside, yet crispy on the outside. It is similar to Sicilian-style pizza, not Chicago-style. Detroit-style is square and the sauce is ladled on after the pizza is baked. Did you know that we have the auto industry to thank for the square shape? Back in the 40s, those steel pans were used in the auto industry to hold nuts and bolts. That is why it is sometimes referred to as "Blue Pan Pizza." Gus Guerra discovered that steel pans, when well-oiled, were great heat conductors and helped to caramelize the cheesy crust. And voila, the Detroit-style pizza was born! I like to make individual pizzas and let my family choose their toppings. Toppings can be put on after the cheese.

SERVES 8

INDIVIDUAL DETROIT-STYLE PIZZAS

Preheat oven to 400°F.

MAKE SAUCE

Cut top third off garlic head, and drizzle garlic cloves with ½ tablespoon of oil. Wrap in foil and place on a baking sheet. Place sliced onions on another piece of foil and drizzle with oil. Wrap up and place on baking sheet, next to garlic. Roast in oven for 45 minutes. Remove baking sheet from oven and increase temperature to 450°F. Open up foil packets, and let garlic and onion cool. In a food processor, add roasted garlic cloves, onion, tomatoes, basil, salt, oregano, granulated garlic and sugar. Process for 2 to 3 minutes, or until well blended. Add mixture to a saucepan and bring to a simmer over medium heat, then reduce the heat to low and keep warm until ready to ladle over pizza.

MAKE CRUST

In a mixing bowl, add flour and salt.

In a small bowl, add yeast and sugar to warm water and whisk together, vigorously, for 30 seconds. Let sit for 10 minutes to activate the yeast. After 10 minutes, you will see some foam on top. Stir again and pour into the mixing bowl with flour. (If you don't see foam, the yeast didn't activate. Throw water out and start the yeast step over; the water temperature is key.)

To mix by hand: Use a well-oiled wooden spoon, and mix until dough forms into a ball.

To mix using a stand mixer with a dough hook: Mix on low for 5 minutes, or until dough comes together.

Add oil to hands and knead dough on a lightly floured surface, about 15 times, or until elastic. Add some oil to the bowl and place dough back in bowl; cover and let rest for 30 minutes.

Lightly butter and oil the bottoms and sides on the inside of 8 mini steel loaf pans. Cut dough into 8 equal pieces. Press dough into bottom of each pan, but don't press dough up the sides. The cheese is the crust for the sides. If dough pulls back, it needs to proof longer. Cover and let rest for 15 minutes or more. Proofing the dough longer will result in a better crust. The dough is ready when it easily presses into all 4 corners of the pan.

ASSEMBLE

Arrange pepperoni slices on top of dough, then sprinkle cheeses over top. Make sure to go all the way to the edges with cheese. The sides on the pizza will be a cheese crust. This is when you can add extra toppings, if you wish.

Bake at 450°F for 13 to 15 minutes, depending on toppings.

Remove pizzas from pans, and ladle sauce over top. Garnish with fresh basil.

BLUE CHEESE DRESSING

- ⅓ cup sour cream
- ⅓ cup mayonnaise
- ¼ cup buttermilk
- 1 teaspoon Worcestershire sauce
- ½ teaspoon House Seasoning (page 96)
- 1 cup crumbled blue cheese
- 1 teaspoon chopped chives

STEAK

- 1 (2½-pound) bone-in ribeye steak, cut 2½ inches thick
- Kosher salt
- Freshly cracked black pepper

WEDGE

- ½ head iceberg lettuce, cored and cut into 2 wedges
- ¼ cup diced Roma tomatoes
- 1 tablespoon chopped red onion
- 4 slices cooked bacon, chopped
- 2 tablespoons blue cheese crumbles

PEPPERCORN SAUCE

- 2 tablespoons butter
- ¼ finely chopped onion
- 1 tablespoon freshly crushed black or green peppercorns
- 2 ounces bourbon
- ⅓ cup beef stock
- ¾ cup heavy cream
- 1½ tablespoons ground mustard
- 1 teaspoon soy sauce

My grandpa always said, "Fat is flavor," and that's exactly why the ribeye is my favorite cut. I always say that I want my last meal to be a Cowboy Ribeye, medium rare, a wedge salad and grilled lemon-pepper asparagus. Throw in some bone marrow with crusty bread, and that's heaven on a plate.

SERVES 2

COWBOY RIBEYE
WITH PEPPERCORN SAUCE AND WEDGE SALAD

Preheat grill to 400°F.

MAKE BLUE CHEESE DRESSING

In a small bowl, whisk together sour cream, mayonnaise, buttermilk, Worcestershire sauce and House Seasoning. Fold in blue cheese crumbles and chives. Cover and refrigerate until ready to assemble.

PREPARE STEAK

Bring steak to room temperature before grilling. Liberally season both sides of steak with salt and pepper. Grill each side for 7 to 8 minutes, then stand steak straight up to sear the edges; flip until all edges are seared. Internal temperature should be at least 120°F when you remove steak from the grill.

Let rest for 15 to 20 minutes on a cutting board.

PREPARE WEDGE SALAD

Top each lettuce wedge with tomatoes, onion, bacon and blue cheese crumbles. Refrigerate until ready to assemble.

MAKE PEPPERCORN SAUCE

In a medium saucepan, add butter and onion, and cook for 4 to 5 minutes over medium heat. Add crushed pepper and bourbon, and cook for 2 to 3 more minutes. Stir in beef stock and cook until it starts to reduce, then whisk in heavy cream, mustard and soy sauce. Simmer until thickened; reduce heat and keep warm.

ASSEMBLE

Drizzle Blue Cheese Dressing over wedge salad. Serve alongside steak and Peppercorn Sauce.

NOTE

I use BLiS Bourbon-Maple Barrel Aged Soy Sauce or BLiS Hardwood Smoked Barrel Aged Soy Sauce for the soy sauce.

To make this steak using the oven, preheat the oven to 400°F. Place steak in a preheated cast-iron skillet over medium-high heat. Add 2 tablespoons of canola oil and sear both sides for 2 minutes each, then sear the edges for 1 more minute. Transfer to oven and cook for 20 to 25 minutes, or until internal temperature reaches 120°F. Remove from oven, then place 2 tablespoons of Garlic-Herb Compound Butter (page 158) on top of steak and let rest for 15 to 20 minutes.

My Grandma Betty was Irish, so I learned to cook a lot of Irish food. I love to add corned beef to just about anything. This Irish Beer Cheese Soup is so good, and when you add the jalapeños it really makes this cheesy soup over-the-top delicious. There are good jalapeño cheeses on the market, so if you don't want it too spicy, simply omit the fresh jalapeños and substitute jalapeño cheese. We are known for our beer here in Michigan, so choose your favorite beer to add to this recipe.

SERVES 4 to 6

JALAPEÑO IRISH BEER CHEESE SOUP

In a saucepan over medium-high heat, whisk together chicken broth, heavy cream and House Seasoning. Bring to a simmer, then reduce heat to low and keep warm.

Add onion and carrots to saucepan and cook over medium heat until translucent, 4 to 5 minutes. Add butter and melt, then add flour and cook for 1 to 2 more minutes. Whisk in beer and cook for 2 to 3 more minutes. Slowly whisk in the warm broth-and-cream mixture. Continue to cook and whisk until soup is thickened. Reduce heat to low, then add cheeses and stir to thoroughly combine. Fold in jalapeños and chopped meat, and keep warm until ready to serve.

Garnish with bacon, croutons and chives.

1½ cups chicken broth

1½ cups heavy cream

½ tablespoon House Seasoning (page 96)

½ cup chopped onion

½ cup diced carrots

4 tablespoons butter

4 tablespoons flour

12 ounces Michigan beer (I use American Badass Lager)

½ cup grated Parmesan cheese

8 ounces shredded sharp white cheddar cheese

8 ounces shredded Gouda cheese

2 tablespoons diced jalapeños

1 cup cooked and chopped corned beef or pastrami

GARNISH

4 slices cooked bacon, chopped

House-Seasoned Croutons (page 160)

Chives

MAMA G'S MEATLOAF
& LOADED POTATO BITES

SERVES 6 to 8

My daughters' friends call me "Mama G." Whenever I would ask them, "What do you guys want to eat?" their favorite reply was usually: "Mama G's Meatloaf and Loaded Potato Bites." And my granddaughter, Cora, would always see these and say, "Look! We're having meat and cupcakes!" I use my House-Seasoned Croutons (page 160) and finely grind them for the breadcrumbs in the meatloaf.

MEATLOAF

- 1½ pounds ground beef
- 1 pound ground pork sausage or chorizo
- 2 eggs, beaten
- ½ cup breadcrumbs
- ¼ cup heavy cream
- ½ cup chopped onion
- ¼ cup chopped bell peppers
- ¼ cup chopped celery
- 2 tablespoons Worcestershire sauce
- 3 tablespoons House Seasoning (page 96)

POTATOES

- 6 medium russet potatoes

GLAZE

- ⅓ cup ketchup
- ¼ cup Concord grape jelly
- ¼ teaspoon smoked paprika

POTATO FILLING

- ⅓ cup sour cream
- 2 tablespoons chopped scallions
- ¼ cup shredded cheese plus extra for garnish
- 2 tablespoons cooked and crumbled bacon
- ¼ cup steamed and chopped broccoli
- ¼ teaspoon House Seasoning (page 96)

Preheat oven to 375°F. Line a large baking sheet with aluminum foil.

PREPARE MEATLOAF

In a large bowl, mix together all meatloaf ingredients until well-incorporated. Do not overmix the meat, or it will become tough. Add mixture to center of baking sheet and form into a rectangular shape, about 2 inches thick. Be sure to leave room around perimeter for potatoes.

PREPARE POTATOES

Wash and dry potatoes, then pierce each one with a fork several times. Place potatoes on baking sheet around meatloaf.

MAKE GLAZE

Whisk together ketchup, jelly and paprika in a small bowl, then set aside.

Bake meat and potatoes for 45 minutes, then turn potatoes over and spread glaze over meatloaf. Continue to bake until meatloaf is thoroughly cooked and potatoes are fork-tender, another 15 to 20 minutes.

MAKE POTATO FILLING

Combine potato-filling ingredients in a medium-size bowl and refrigerate until ready to assemble.

ASSEMBLE

Remove meatloaf from baking sheet and add to a large serving dish, then lightly tent with foil. Cut each potato in half, then cut the ends off each half so the potato bite will stand straight up. Scoop out some potato from each half to form a well (I use a mellon baller), then mash the excess potato in a small bowl. Add the mashed potato to the potato-filling mixture and spoon the mixture back into the potato bites. Place potato bites on a clean baking sheet, sprinkle with extra cheese and bake for 5 minutes. Serve warm alongside meatloaf.

Forget Taco Tuesdays; we love tacos every day. Tacos are too good for just one day, and this recipe is seriously the best. I prefer to use chicken thighs instead of breasts because they're so much juicier and more flavorful. I also prefer corn tortillas over flour, and slaw instead of plain lettuce. My family loves spicy food, so I make a Creamy Harissa once a month and keep it in the fridge. Harissa is a red-pepper chili paste that adds the perfect punch to these tacos, but you can use Sriracha or other bottled hot sauce.

SERVES 6 to 8

MESQUITE LIME CHICKEN TACOS

SLAW

- ⅓ cup mayonnaise
- 2 tablespoons apple cider vinegar
- ¼ cup sugar
- ¼ teaspoon celery seed
- ¼ teaspoon salt
- ⅛ teaspoon pepper
- 2 cups shredded cabbage
- 1 cup shredded red cabbage
- ½ cup matchstick carrots
- ½ cup thinly sliced radishes

CREAMY HARISSA

- ½ cup sour cream
- 2 tablespoons Harissa (recipe on facing page or substitute store bought)

LIME CHICKEN

- 2 tablespoons vegetable oil
- 8 boneless, skinless chicken thighs
- 2 teaspoons House Seasoning (page 96)
- 1 teaspoon mesquite seasoning
- Juice of 1 lime

- 16-ounce package corn tortillas, warmed
- 2 cups crumbled cotija cheese

GARNISH

- Fresh cilantro
- Lime wedges

PREPARE SLAW

In a small bowl, whisk together mayonnaise, vinegar, sugar, celery seed, salt and pepper. Add cabbage, carrots and radishes to dressing and toss together. Refrigerate until ready to assemble.

MAKE CREAMY HARISSA

In a small bowl, whisk together sour cream and Harissa. Refrigerate until ready to assemble.

PREPARE CHICKEN

Heat oil in a large skillet over medium-high heat. Season both sides of chicken thighs with House Seasoning and mesquite seasoning. Place thighs in skillet and cook for 3 to 4 minutes per side, or until thoroughly cooked. Let rest, then shred or cube the meat. Add meat and juices back into the skillet to keep warm, then add lime juice.

ASSEMBLE

Place equal amounts of chicken, slaw and creamy harissa on each tortilla. Garnish with cilantro and lime wedges.

MAKE HARISSA

Preheat oven to 425°F. Roast bell peppers, skin-side up, for 30 minutes. Let peppers cool, then remove the outer skin.

Place chili peppers in a bowl and add hot water to rehydrate for 30 minutes. Drain and set aside.

Add coriander, caraway, cumin and celery seeds to a small skillet and toast for 3 to 4 minutes over medium-low heat. Add toasted seeds to a mortar and pestle or spice grinder and finely grind.

Place roasted peppers and remaining ingredients in a food processor. Process to form a paste, scraping down the sides of the container as necessary. Transfer paste to an airtight jar and add the 2 tablespoons of olive oil on top; refrigerate for up to 3 weeks.

HARISSA

- 3 red bell peppers, stemmed, halved and seeded
- 2 ounces ancho chili peppers, stemmed and seeded
- 2 ounces guajillo chili peppers, stemmed and seeded
- 1½ teaspoons coriander seeds
- 1 teaspoon caraway seeds
- 1 teaspoon cumin seeds
- 1 teaspoon celery seeds
- 1½ teaspoons salt
- 4 cloves garlic
- ½ cup olive oil plus 2 tablespoons for sealing jar at the end
- 2 tablespoons red wine vinegar
- Juice of 1 lemon
- 1 tablespoon honey

Macaroni and cheese is the ultimate comfort food and crowd-pleaser. In fact, I don't think I've ever met anyone who doesn't like it. I sometimes add ham and peas if I'm trying to make it a full dinner meal. My favorite mac and cheese in the entire world is at Clarkston Union in Clarkston, Michigan. But this recipe is a very close second if you can't make it to Clarkston. (If you do go, also get their ribs!)

SERVES 6

MITTEN MAC-N-CHEESE

Preheat oven to 350°F. Spray a 9-by-13-inch baking dish with nonstick cooking spray.

PREPARE PASTA

Cook pasta according to package directions, then drain and set aside.

MAKE CHEESE SAUCE

In a saucepan over medium-high heat, whisk together milk, heavy cream, House Seasoning and nutmeg. Bring to a simmer, then reduce heat to low and keep warm.

In a large saucepan, add butter and onion, and cook over medium heat for 4 to 5 minutes. Add garlic and cook for 1 more minute. Stir in flour and continue to cook for 2 more minutes. Slowly add cream mixture, whisking continually. Once the mixture thickens, stir in ½ cup yellow sharp cheese and all other cheeses, and remove from heat. Add to pasta and stir to combine.

MAKE TOPPING

In a small bowl, mix together breadcrumbs and melted butter.

ASSEMBLE

Pour cheesy pasta into baking dish. Sprinkle remaining ½ cup yellow sharp cheddar cheese and topping evenly over pasta, then bake for 35 to 40 minutes. Serve warm. Garnish with scallions and tomatoes, if desired.

---

1 pound cavatappi pasta

CHEESE SAUCE

2 cups milk

1½ cups heavy cream

1 tablespoon House Seasoning (page 96)

⅛ teaspoon freshly grated nutmeg

¼ cup butter

½ cup chopped onion

2 cloves garlic, grated

¼ cup flour

1 cup freshly shredded yellow sharp cheddar cheese, divided use

1 cup freshly shredded white sharp cheddar cheese

1 cup freshly shredded Pinconning cheese (subsititute: Colby cheese)

½ cup freshly grated Parmesan cheese

TOPPING

1 cup panko breadcrumbs

¼ cup melted butter

GARNISH

Chopped scallions

Chopped tomatoes

- 2 pounds boneless chuck roast, cubed
- 1 tablespoon crushed black peppercorns
- 2 teaspoons salt, divided use
- 2 tablespoons olive oil
- 2 tablespoons BLiS Hardwood Smoked Barrel Aged Soy Sauce, divided use

RAGU

- 3 tablespoons butter
- 1 cup chopped onion
- 3 cloves garlic, minced
- ¾ cup diced celery
- ¾ cup diced carrots
- ½ cup diced bell peppers
- 1 (6-ounce) can tomato paste
- ¾ cup red wine
- 1 (28-ounce) can diced tomatoes
- 1¼ cups beef stock
- 2 bay leaves
- 1½ teaspoons chopped fresh thyme leaves

- 1 pound pappardelle pasta

GARNISH

- Freshly grated Parmesan cheese
- Ricotta
- Fresh basil leaves

NOTE

BLiS Gourmet is a Michigan-based sauce company. You can order their soy sauce at *blisgourmet.com*, or substitute 1 tablespoon soy sauce, 1 tablespoon bourbon and ⅛ teaspoon liquid smoke.

You may have noticed from my recipes throughout this book that I love pepper! I'll pepper-crust anything I can get my hands on. One of my favorite things to make on a Sunday afternoon, especially if we are snowed-in, is this beef ragu. It is a warm bowl of love for your soul. Think of snow lightly falling, the fireplace lit, this beef ragu on the stove and a glass of red wine in hand—that is a perfect way to spend a wintry day in Michigan.

SERVES 6 to 8

PAPPARDELLE PEPPER-CRUSTED BEEF RAGU

Evenly coat cubed meat with crushed peppercorns and 1 teaspoon of salt.

PREPARE BEEF

In a large stockpot or Dutch oven, heat oil over medium-high heat. Add the seasoned meat and brown all sides, about 2 to 3 minutes per side. Stir in 1 tablespoon of soy sauce. Using a slotted spoon, remove meat and place in a bowl.

MAKE RAGU

Add butter to hot oil, then add onion and cook until translucent, about 4 to 5 minutes. Add garlic, celery, carrots and peppers, and cook for 4 to 5 minutes.

Add meat back to stockpot or Dutch oven, then stir in tomato paste. Add wine, tomatoes and beef stock. Stir everything together and bring to a simmer. Add bay leaves, thyme and remaining salt. Cover and reduce heat to low for 2 to 3 hours, or until meat is fork-tender.

PREPARE PASTA

Cook pasta al dente, according to package instructions. Drain and set aside.

ASSEMBLE

Remove bay leaves and stir in remaining soy sauce, then fold pasta into meat sauce. Top each serving with Parmesan cheese, a dollop of ricotta and fresh basil leaves. Serve warm.

Since a grilled cheese and tomato soup should never be apart, I decided to combine them in the same bowl. The cheddar cheese crisps are super easy to make and don't harden like a Parmesan crisp. Combined with my homemade croutons, they act like the grilled cheese in this soup. If I'm feeling a little more indulgent, I'll add a little heavy cream, a Parmesan rind or I'll even add some vodka, cream and penne pasta.

SERVES 4 to 6

TOMATO BASIL SOUP
WITH CHEDDAR CHEESE CRISPS

- 3 tablespoons olive oil
- 1 cup chopped sweet onion
- 3 cloves garlic, minced
- 1 cup chicken stock
- 1 (28-ounce) can crushed tomatoes
- 1 tablespoon tomato paste
- 1½ tablespoons sugar
- 2 tablespoons fresh basil, plus extra for garnish
- ½ teaspoon dried oregano
- 2 teaspoons House Seasoning (page 96)
- ¼ teaspoon red-pepper flakes (optional)

CHEDDAR CHEESE CRISPS

- 8 ounces freshly shredded cheddar cheese

GARNISH

House-Seasoned Croutons (page 160)

Preheat oven to 325°F. Line a baking sheet with a silicone mat or parchment paper.

MAKE SOUP

Add olive oil and onion to a large saucepan or Dutch oven and cook over medium heat for 4 to 5 minutes, or until translucent. Add garlic and cook for 30 more seconds, stirring continually. Add chicken stock, crushed tomatoes, tomato paste, sugar, basil, oregano, House Seasoning and red-pepper flakes, if using. Stir together and cook for 18 to 20 minutes.

Using an immersion blender, blend soup together until desired consistency. Simmer on low until ready to serve. (Note: If using a blender, add soup in small batches and blend together. Don't overfill or soup will spill over the sides.)

MAKE CHEESE CRISPS

Place 2 tablespoons of shredded cheese on the baking sheet, form into a round and gently pat down. Repeat this process for the remaining cheese, keeping space between each round. Bake for 2 to 3 minutes, then cool for at least 5 minutes before removing. Lift each round with a spatula and roll up. Place each rolled-up round, seam-side down, back on the backing sheet until ready to assemble.

ASSEMBLE

Add soup to bowls and garnish with croutons, cheese rounds and fresh basil.

This cake won me top honors on *Good Morning America* on National Chocolate Cake Day (yes, there is such a thing). I love the sweet and salty combination in this cake, and, luckily, so did the judges on GMA, including celebrity chef Rocco DiSpirito.

SERVES 12

PRETZEL CRUSTED CHOCOLATE CAKE
WITH PEANUT BUTTER FROSTING

PRETZEL CRUST
2 cups pretzels, finely crushed
½ cup sugar
1 cup butter, melted
1 egg, beaten

CHOCOLATE CAKE
1¾ cups flour
½ teaspoon salt
¾ cup cocoa powder
1 teaspoon baking soda
2 cups sugar
½ cup butter, softened
2 eggs, room temperature
2 teaspoons vanilla extract
¾ cup milk
1 cup hot French vanilla coffee

FROSTING
8 ounces cream cheese, softened
1 cup powdered sugar
1 cup peanut butter
½ tablespoon vanilla extract
½ cup milk

NOTE
Feel free to line the entire pan with parchment paper beforehand. When the cake is done baking, it will be easy to pull out, frost and cut.

Preheat oven to 350°F. Spray a 9-by-13-inch pan with nonstick cooking spray.

MAKE PRETZEL CRUST

In a medium bowl, mix together pretzels, sugar, butter and egg. Add to the bottom of the pan, and press down for even distribution.

MAKE CHOCOLATE CAKE

In a medium bowl, sift together flour, salt, cocoa powder and baking soda. Set aside.

Using an electric mixer with a paddle attachment, cream together sugar and butter on high speed until creamy. Turn the mixer to low and slowly add eggs, vanilla and milk. Beat for 2 to 3 minutes. Add the dry ingredients and beat until thoroughly combined, then slowly pour in the hot coffee. Scrape down the sides, as necessary. Continue to mix until all ingredients are well incorporated.

Pour the cake mixture over the pretzel crust and bake for 50 to 60 minutes, or until a toothpick inserted into the center comes out clean. Let cool.

MAKE FROSTING

Combine all frosting ingredients together, and beat until creamy.

ASSEMBLE

Frost the cake when cooled, then cut into desired servings. Refrigerate the remaining pieces of cake.

My Ritzy Rich Bars are decadent, buttery and delicious. They are a shortbread-cookie cheesecake turtle bar. The best part? The crust is made of finely ground Ritz crackers instead of flour. These are amazing and delicious!

SERVES 12

RITZY RICH BARS
SHORTBREAD-COOKIE CHEESECAKE TURTLE BARS

SHORTBREAD CRUST

2 sticks unsalted butter, softened

½ cup sugar

2 cups finely ground Ritz® crackers (approximately 2 sleeves)

1 teaspoon vanilla extract

CHEESECAKE

2 (8-ounce) packages cream cheese, softened

1 cup sugar

¾ cup sour cream

2 eggs, room temperature

½ cup flour

2 teaspoons vanilla extract

TOPPING

¼ cup caramel

¼ chocolate syrup or hot fudge

¼ cup chopped pecans

Preheat oven to 325°F. Line a 9-by-13-inch pan with parchment paper.

MAKE SHORTBREAD CRUST

Using an electric stand mixer with a paddle attachment, cream together butter and sugar on high speed until creamy. Add crackers and vanilla, and continue to beat together until thoroughly combined. Press mixture into lined pan, and press down for even distribution.

MAKE CHEESECAKE

Cream together cream cheese and sugar until light and fluffy. Add sour cream, eggs, flour and vanilla until well-combined. Spread cheesecake mixture over shortbread cookie crust and bake on the bottom rack for 45 minutes, then transfer to the top rack and bake for 5 to 10 more minutes, or until a toothpick inserted into the center comes out clean.

ASSEMBLE

Cool the cheesecake in the refrigerator for at least 3 hours. When ready to serve, drizzle with caramel, chocolate syrup or hot fudge and pecans. Cut into 12 bars. Refrigerate any leftovers.

ACKNOWLEDGMENTS

I'm a firm believer in putting God first, family second and career third. When I keep these priorities in order, life is bliss. When these get out of order, then life is chaotic. Thank you, Dear Lord, for always being there for me. For being my savior and my mentor, and for your amazing grace. Without you, I am nothing!

THANK YOU TO MY FAMILY AND FRIENDS:
To my mom, for having delicious meals prepared every night at 5:30 when I was growing up and for making everyone sit down at the table together.

To my dad Lloyd for having an amazing garden and bringing fresh produce to me all summer long.

To my dad Leo for always being there and supporting me in everything that I do.

To my husband, Ted, for your constant support and dedication to our family. You'll pretty much eat anything, except liver, and I appreciate that. Love you!

To my daughter Ariana for being so patient—even when you were studying for your master's—with every photo and recipe that I sent to you asking A, B or C. I truly don't know what I would do without your love and support. Love you, Ari!

To my daughter Andrea and son-in-law, Derrick, for all of your support. Whether it's a video shoot, photo shoot or eating countless meals for recipe testing, thanks for being willing participants. Love you guys!

To my granddaughter, Cora, for being my meat-loving girl. (When she comes over to GiGi & PaPa's house, she loves to help in the kitchen, and she loves to sing karaoke with me.) GiGi loves you, Cora.

To my brother, Damon, for always being there for me. And I know Todd is with us, every day. Thanks to my niece, Isabelle. You are an amazing young woman, and you are becoming quite the cook. I love that!

To my sister, Dana, for always being willing to cook with me! I am so happy when we are in the kitchen together and making memories. To my nephews Cody and Logan for always loving my burgers. And to Greg for always opening his home—and kitchen—to us.

To my Uncle Dave at Krantz Farms, for your endless supply of fruits and vegetables from the farm anytime I need them for recipes or TV segments.

To my best friend, Anna Duggins, her husband, Greg, and my two godsons, Jack and George. Thanks, Anna, for being my everything since fifth grade.

To Rhonda and Scott Greiner at Greiner Farms, for your friendship, encouragement and support. You guys are like our second family. Thanks for all the fresh produce over the years.

To Ty and Robin Bradley, for your friendship and for introducing me to the Muffpot one winter while snowmobiling. Our snowmobile trips have never been the same.

To Ted and Banda Trocke, for all the fresh herbs from your garden. My food styling and food photography wouldn't be pretty without your beautiful herbs. And thank you for delivering them as well.

To Fuehring Family Farms, for always providing me fresh fruits and vegetables to use in my recipes.

To the Oomen and Kokx families, for providing great produce for my TV segments.

To David Hackert, for allowing us to use your cherry orchard to shoot the cherry blossom photos for the book.

To Todd and Kellie Fox at Fox Barn Market & Winery, for providing years of wine and produce for me to use for recipes and TV segments.

To Dave and Leslie Hansen at Hansen Foods, for always providing me with new products and for ordering specialty items whenever needed.

To Todd and Sarah Greiner at Todd Greiner Farms, for the fresh asparagus to use on my TV segments.

To Pat Gamble, for giving me my first cookbook. (I would deliver homemade chocolate chip cookies to her when I was in high school and college. She gave me a variety cookie cookbook—guess she was sick of chocolate chips!)

THANK YOU TO EVERYONE WHO HAS HELPED ME IN MY CAREER:

To my loyal readers and followers of Nom News — Boating, Boarding and Burgers. Without your encouragement and support, I wouldn't be writing this cookbook. Thanks to everyone who

pre-ordered the book and believed in me.

To the crew at Wave Club Water Sports and Wet Head Beach Shop. I have been happy to cook and grill for our employees; it has been my pleasure. I feel privileged to have worked with you guys for the past 25 years. Here's to another 25.

A huge thank you to the entire team at Story Farm. Thanks, Bob and Bo Morris, for making this book a reality. Thank you to my editor, Ashley Fraxedas, for being so amazing. I knew after our first conversation that we would be instant friends, and when we met for the first time touring wineries in Old Mission, I knew you'd be a lifelong friend. Thanks to my art director, Jason Farmand, for making this book so beautiful.

To Lisa Ekus, for your time and guidance when I was thinking about writing my first cookbook.

Thank you for introducing me to the Story Farm team. It was a perfect match!

To Todd & Brad Reed Photography, for your stunning photography of Michigan landscapes. Thank you for allowing me to use your amazing seasonal photos for chapter openers.

To Josh and Jamie Schexnaildre at Slow Juke Photography, for your vision and beautiful photos from the Sleeping Bear Dunes and winery shoots.

To John Bakker and the Michigan Asparagus Advisory Board, for allowing me to work with you to create recipes and to support our local farmers.

To Riveridge, for your fresh fruits and vegetables for my recipes and TV segments. I appreciate those early morning deliveries to the TV station so that we could show the freshest produce possible.

To Tracy Forner (co-host of *Indy Style*) and the team at WISH-TV, for having me on year after year to show my Michigan asparagus recipes and support Michigan asparagus.

To Bonobo Winery, for allowing us to shoot photos of your gorgeous winery and delicious wine.

To *Good Morning America*, for flying me to New York City to compete in the National Chocolate Cake Day contest. Thank you to Jesse Palmer, Amy Robach, Lara Spencer and Lily James for hosting the segment and for making my first national appearance on TV an amazing experience. Thanks to Karen Pickus for the great food styling. Thank you to the New York–New Jersey Bakers Club for judging the competition. And a huge thanks to Rocco DiSpirito for choosing this Michigander to win!

To John Gonzalez at MLive, for publishing some amazing food articles on my GMA journey and beyond.

To Allison Scarborough at Oceana County Press, for your support and for covering my food journeys and businesses.

To the *Jeep Talk Show* family and listeners. Thanks Josh, Tony and Tammy. I love being a food and travel contributor with the *Jeep Talk Show*.

To the food team at the *Today* show. Thank you for featuring more than 20 of my recipes on your food emails and website. I appreciate the food features over the years.

To ABC's *The Chew*, the Food Network & Cooking Channel New York City Wine & Food Festival (NYCWFF), *The Rachael Ray Show* and Hallmark's *Home & Family* program, for the features.

And last but not least, a HUGE thank you to my WZZM TV-13 family in Grand Rapids, Michigan. Thank you to Denise Pritchard, for giving me my first TV food segment. Without that segment, I wouldn't have ever created a food blog. So, you're the one to either thank or blame. Haha, just kidding! I will be forever grateful. And thank you to Stephanie Webb, for being the reporter on that first segment and for making it so easy for me. (And for having me on your stations in Florida, after you moved.) Also, thanks to Lauren Stanton, Val Lego, Meredith TerHaar, Catherine Behrendt and Rhonda Ross. You guys have supported me over the years, and have had me on time and time again to show my recipes and support my upcoming cookbook. Thanks to the entire WZZM family—love you all!

INDEX

Page numbers in italics indicate photos.

A

Ancho Chile Asparagus Guacamole, 42, *43*
Antipasto Salad with Bloody Mary Vinaigrette, *120,* 121
appetizers
    Deluxe Tater Tot Bites, *138,* 139
    Roasted and Toasted Tomato Crostini, 114, *115*
    Spinach & Artichoke Bacon Bread Bowl, 134–135, *135*
apples
    Apple and Onion Pulled Pork Sandwiches & Nachos, 122, *123*
    Apple Cider Moscow Mules with Caramel Apple Cheesecake Skewers, 24, *25*
    Apple Cinnamon Loaded Sweet Potatoes, 146, *147*
    Apple Crisp Ice Cream Pie Topped with Salted Caramel Frosted Flakes, 166, *167*
    Apple Fritter Dip, *142,* 143
"appy tails"
    about, 21
    Apple Cider Moscow Mules with Caramel Apple Cheesecake Skewers, 24, *25*
    Blackberry Mojitos with Salami, Mint & Mozzarella Skewers, *26,* 27
    Black Cherry Mimosas with Triple Cherry Brownie Bite Skewers, *22,* 23
    Blue Cheese Rimmed Bloody Mary-Tini, 28, *29*
    Dune Docker Cocktails with Coconut Shrimp Skewers, 30–31, *31*
    Golden Cadillac Shakes with Chocolate Ganache & Graham Cracker-Toffee S'more Skewers, *32,* 33
    Michigan Manhattan Cocktails with Ancho Chili Candied Bacon & Bourbon-Soaked Black Cherries Skewer, 34, *35*
    Peach Bellinis with Mozzarella, Basil & Prosciutto Peach Skewers, *36,* 37
    Silver Sunset Cocktails—Jalapeño Pineapple Margaritas & Filet Mignon Kabobs, 38, *39*
asparagus
    Ancho Chile Asparagus Guacamole, 42, *43*
    Asparagus Crust White Chicken Pizza, 48, *49*
    Asparagus & Havarti Dill Sheet Pan Eggs, *50,* 51
    Asparagus Spring Salad in Parmesan Cheese Cups, 52, *53*
    Deep-Fried Asparagus Roll-Ups with Chipotle Lime Dipping Sauce, 44, *45*
    Soba Noodle Asparagus Chicken Satay, 54, *55*
    Spring Morel Risotto with Asparagus & Peas, *60,* 61
    Teriyaki Pineapple Chicken with Asparagus in a Pineapple Bowl, *56,* 57
avocados
    Ancho Chile Asparagus Guacamole, 42, *43*
    Buffalo Chicken Quinoa Burgers on Avocado Toast, 88–89, *89*
    Gold Coast Grilled Cheese—Beer-Battered Avocado Grilled Cheese with Chipotle Peach Slaw, 84, *85*
    Shakin' Chipotle Cherry Burgers with Peach Mimosa Salsa & Adobo Avocado Aioli on Pretzel Buns, 74–75, *75*
    Sweet Smell of Summer Burgers—Thyme-Infused

Teriyaki Burgers with Pineapple Salsa & Guacamole, 70–71, *71*

B

bacon
    Ancho Chili Candied Bacon & Bourbon-Soaked Black Cherries Skewers, 34, *35*
    Buffalo Chicken Grilled Cheese/Wedge BLT, *80,* 81
    Spinach & Artichoke Bacon Bread Bowl, 134–135, *135*

bars and brownies
    Pecan Pumpkin Bars with Maple Cream Cheese Frosting, *168,* 169
    Ritzy Rich Bars—Shortbread-Cookie Cheesecake Turtle Bars, 196, *197*
    Scotchie Squash Cheesecake Bars, 170–171, *171*
    Triple Cherry Brownies, 116, *117*

beef
    about grinding, 77
    Boating & Boarding Burgers, *86,* 87
    Campfire Coney Dogs, *126,* 127
    Caprese Burgers with Pistachio Pesto & Blueberry Balsamic Drizzle, *82,* 83
    Cowboy Ribeye with Peppercorn Sauce and Wedge Salad, 180, *181*
    Croissant Croque-Madame Burgers, 78–79, *79*
    Defend the Den Burgers Topped with Jalapeño Onion Poppers & Zesty Sauce, 72–73, *73*
    Deluxe Tater Tot Bites, *138,* 139
    Filet Mignon Kabobs, 38, *39*
    Game Day Sloppy Joes, *128,* 129
    Mama G's Meatloaf & Loaded Potato Bites, 184–185, *185*
    Mighty Mac Olive Burger, *68,* 69
    Muffler Meatballs, 130, *131*
    Pappardelle Pepper-Crusted Beef Ragu, 190, *191*
    Peach Habanero Mini Burgers, *76,* 77
    Pepper-Crusted Pastrami Burgers, 66, *67*
    Shakin' Chipotle Cherry Burgers with Peach Mimosa Salsa & Adobo Avocado Aioli on Pretzel Buns, 74–75, *75*
    Sweet Smell of Summer Burgers—Thyme-Infused Teriyaki Burgers with Pineapple Salsa & Guacamole, 70–71, *71*

beer
    Beer-Battered Avocado Grilled Cheese with Chipotle Peach Slaw, 84, *85*
    Jalapeño Irish Beer Cheese Soup, *182,* 183

Blackberry Mojitos with Salami, Mint & Mozzarella Skewers, *26,* 27

Black Cherry Mimosas with Triple Cherry Brownie Bite Skewers, *22,* 23

blueberries
    Buttermilk Blueberry Breakfast Cake, 92, *93*
    Caprese Burgers with Pistachio Pesto & Blueberry Balsamic Drizzle, *82,* 83
    Cherry-Berry Stuffed French Toast Casserole, 98, *99*

Blue Cheese Rimmed Bloody Mary-Tini, 28, *29*

Boating & Boarding Burgers, *86,* 87

bread
    Apple Fritter Dip, *142,* 143
    Cherry-Berry Stuffed French Toast Casserole, 98, *99*
    Dried Cranberry Sage Stuffing, 160, *161*
    Holiday Breakfast Casserole, 174, *175*
    Roasted and Toasted Tomato Crostini, 114, *115*
    Spinach & Artichoke Bacon Bread Bowl, 134–135, *135*

breakfast and brunch
    Buttermilk Blueberry Breakfast Cake, 92, *93*
    Cheesy Ham & Pepper Egg Cups, *94,* 95
    Cherry-Berry Stuffed French Toast Casserole, 98, *99*
    Holiday Breakfast Casserole, 174, *175*
    Brussels Sprouts, GG's, *162,* 163
    Buffalo Chicken Grilled Cheese/Wedge BLT, *80,* 81
    Buffalo Chicken Quinoa Burgers on Avocado Toast, 88–89, *89*

burgers & sammies
    about, 65
    Apple and Onion Pulled Pork Sandwiches & Nachos, 122, *123*
    Boating & Boarding Burgers, *86,* 87
    Buffalo Chicken Grilled Cheese/Wedge BLT, *80,* 81
    Buffalo Chicken Quinoa Burgers on Avocado Toast, 88–89, *89*
    Campfire Coney Dogs, *126,* 127
    Caprese Burgers with Pistachio Pesto & Blueberry Balsamic Drizzle, *82,* 83
    Croissant Croque-Madame Burgers, 78–79, *79*
    Defend the Den Burgers Topped with Jalapeño Onion Poppers & Zesty Sauce, 72–73, *73*
    Game Day Sloppy Joes, *128,* 129
    Gold Coast Grilled Cheese—Beer-Battered Avocado Grilled Cheese with Chipotle Peach Slaw, 84, *85*
    Mighty Mac Olive Burger, *68,* 69
    Peach Habanero Mini Burgers,

76, 77
Pepper-Crusted Pastrami Burgers, 66, 67
Shakin' Chipotle Cherry Burgers with Peach Mimosa Salsa & Adobo Avocado Aioli on Pretzel Buns, 74–75, 75
Sweet Smell of Summer Burgers—Thyme-Infused Teriyaki Burgers with Pineapple Salsa & Guacamole, 70–71, 71
Buttermilk Blueberry Breakfast Cake, 92, 93
Butternut Brown Sugar Quinoa Bowl, 156–157, 157

C

cake
- Buttermilk Blueberry Breakfast Cake, 92, 93
- Pretzel Crusted Chocolate Cake with Peanut Butter Frosting, 194–195, 195

Campfire Coney Dogs, 126, 127
Canoe Corn Lake Bake, 96, 97
Caprese Burgers with Pistachio Pesto & Blueberry Balsamic Drizzle, 82, 83
Charcuterie Board Picnic, 124–125, 125

cheese
- Asparagus Crust White Chicken Pizza, 48, 49
- Buffalo Chicken Grilled Cheese/Wedge BLT, 80, 81
- Caprese Burgers with Pistachio Pesto & Blueberry Balsamic Drizzle, 82, 83
- Cheddar Cheese Crisps, Tomato Basil Soup with, 192
- Cheesy Enchiladas, 176, 177
- Cheesy Ham & Pepper Egg Cups, 94, 95
- Croissant Croque-Madame Burgers, 78–79, 79
- Detroit-Style Pizzas, Individual, 178–179, 179
- Eggplant Parmesan with Sun-Dried Tomato Pesto Sauce, 150–151, 151
- Gold Coast Grilled Cheese—Beer-Battered Avocado Grilled Cheese with Chipotle Peach Slaw, 84, 85
- Havarti Dill & Asparagus Sheet Pan Eggs, 50
- Jalapeño Irish Beer Cheese Soup, 182, 183
- Mitten Mac-N-Cheese, 188, 189
- Parmesan Cheese Cups, Asparagus Spring Salad in, 52, 53
- Pepperoni Pizza Zucchini Boats, 104, 105
- Spinach & Artichoke Bacon Bread Bowl, 134–135, 135
- Strawberry Feta Spinach Salad, 58, 59

cherries
- Black Cherry Mimosas with Triple Cherry Brownie Bite Skewers, 23
- Cherry-Berry Stuffed French Toast Casserole, 98, 99
- cherry season, 12–13, 91
- Grilled Cherry-Chipotle Pork Tenderloin with Cherry Salsa, 106–107, 107
- Michigan Cherry Salad with Maple-Cayenne Candied Walnuts and Cherry-Balsamic Vinaigrette, 108, 109
- Michigan Manhattan Cocktails with Ancho Chili Candied Bacon & Bourbon-Soaked Black Cherries Skewers, 34, 35
- Triple Cherry Brownies, 116, 117

chicken
- Asparagus Crust White Chicken Pizza, 48, 49
- Buffalo Chicken Grilled Cheese/Wedge BLT, 80, 81
- Buffalo Chicken Quinoa Burgers on Avocado Toast, 88–89, 89
- Cheesy Enchiladas, 176, 177
- Chicken Pot Pie Spaghetti Squash, 148, 149
- Garlicky Mushroom Stuffed Roast Chicken, 158–159, 159
- Garlic Scape Stuffed Chicken Breast, 102–103, 103
- Mesquite Lime Chicken Tacos, 186–187, 187
- Soba Noodle Asparagus Chicken Satay, 54, 55
- Swiss Chicken Pasta Salad, 46, 47
- Teriyaki Pineapple Chicken with Asparagus in a Pineapple Bowl, 56, 57

chiles
- Ancho Chile Asparagus Guacamole, 42, 43
- Ancho Chili Candied Bacon & Bourbon-Soaked Black Cherries Skewers, 34, 35
- Deep-Fried Asparagus Roll-Ups with Chipotle Lime Dipping Sauce, 44, 45
- Defend the Den Burgers Topped with Jalapeño Onion Poppers & Zesty Sauce, 72–73, 73
- Green Bean Casserole Topped with Jalapeño Onion Poppers, 164–165, 165
- Grilled Cherry-Chipotle Pork Tenderloin with Cherry Salsa, 106–107, 107
- Jalapeño Irish Beer Cheese Soup, 182, 183
- Peach Habanero Mini Burgers, 76, 77
- Silver Sunset Cocktails—Jalapeño Pineapple Margaritas & Filet

Mignon Kabobs, 38, *39*
Chili, Turkey, 140, *141*
chocolate
    Pretzel Crusted Chocolate Cake with Peanut Butter Frosting, 194–195, *195*
    Triple Cherry Brownies, *116,* 117
cocktails
    Apple Cider Moscow Mules, 24, *25*
    Blackberry Mojitos, *26,* 27
    Black Cherry Mimosas, *22,* 23
    Blue Cheese Rimmed Bloody Mary-Tini, 28, *29*
    Dune Docker Cocktails, 30
    Golden Cadillac Shakes, *32,* 33
    Jalapeño Pineapple Margaritas, 38, *39*
    Michigan Manhattan Cocktails, 34, *35*
    Peach Bellinis, *36,* 37
corn
    Canoe Corn Lake Bake, *96,* 97
Cowboy Ribeye with Peppercorn Sauce and Wedge Salad, 180, *181*
crisps and crumbles
    Apple Crisp Ice Cream Pie Topped with Salted Caramel Frosted Flakes, 166, *167*
    Rhubarb & Strawberry Pretzel Crumble, 62, *63*
Croissant Croque-Madame Burgers, 78–79, *79*
Crostini, Roasted and Toasted Tomato, 114, *115*

D

Deep-Fried Asparagus Roll-Ups with Chipotle Lime Dipping Sauce, 44, *45*
Defend the Den Burgers Topped with Jalapeño Onion Poppers & Zesty Sauce, 72–73, *73*
Deluxe Tater Tot Bites, *138,* 139

desserts and sweets
    Apple Crisp Ice Cream Pie Topped with Salted Caramel Frosted Flakes, 166, *167*
    Apple Fritter Dip, *142,* 143
    Pecan Pumpkin Bars with Maple Cream Cheese Frosting, *168,* 169
    Pretzel Crusted Chocolate Cake with Peanut Butter Frosting, 194–195, *195*
    Rhubarb & Strawberry Pretzel Crumble, 62, *63*
    Ritzy Rich Bars—Shortbread-Cookie Cheesecake Turtle Bars, 196, *197*
    Salted Caramel Peanut Butter Toffee Dip, *132,* 133
    Scotchie Squash Cheesecake Bars, 170–171, *171*
    Triple Cherry Brownies, *116,* 117
Detroit-Style Pizzas, Individual, 178–179, *179*
Dill Pickles, Quick, 110, *111*
dips and spreads
    Ancho Chile Asparagus Guacamole, 42, *43*
    Apple Fritter Dip, *142,* 143
    Chipotle Lime Dipping Sauce, Deep-Fried Asparagus Roll-Ups with, 44, *45*
    Salted Caramel Peanut Butter Toffee Dip, *132,* 133
    Spinach & Artichoke Bacon Bread Bowl, 134–135, *135*
Dried Cranberry Sage Stuffing, 160, *161*

E

Eggplant Parmesan with Sun-Dried Tomato Pesto Sauce, 150–151, *151*
eggs
    Asparagus & Havarti Dill Sheet Pan Eggs, *50,* 51
    Cheesy Ham & Pepper Egg Cups, *94,* 95
    Croissant Croque-Madame Burgers, 78–79, *79*
    Holiday Breakfast Casserole, 174, *175*
Enchiladas, Cheesy, *176,* 177

F

Fall Harvest Salad, 152, *153*
Ferwerda, Gina
    childhood memories, 12–15
    family recipe compilation, 16–17
    Nom News blog, 15
    TV appearances, 15–16
fish and seafood
    Coconut Shrimp Skewers, 30–31, *31*
    Steelhead Trout in Parchment, 136, *137*
    Watermelon Radish and Romanesco Salmon Salad, *154,* 155
French Toast Casserole, Cherry-Berry Stuffed, 98, *99*
fruit. *See also* specific fruits
    Cherry-Berry Stuffed French Toast Casserole, 98, *99*
    Grilled Fruit Salad, *100,* 101
    Rhubarb & Strawberry Pretzel Crumble, 62, *63*

G

Game Day Sloppy Joes, *128,* 129
Garlicky Mushroom Stuffed Roast Chicken, 158–159, *159*
Garlic Scape Stuffed Chicken Breast, 102–103, *103*
GG's Brussels Sprouts, *162,* 163
Gold Coast Grilled Cheese—Beer-Battered Avocado Grilled Cheese with Chipotle Peach Slaw, 84, *85*
Golden Cadillac Shakes with Chocolate Ganache & Graham Cracker-Toffee S'more Skewers, *32,* 33
green beans

Canoe Corn Lake Bake, 96, *97*
Green Bean Casserole Topped with Jalapeño Onion Poppers, 164–165, *165*
Summer Veggie Pasta, *112,* 113

greens
Fall Harvest Salad, 152, *153*
Grilled Cherry-Chipotle Pork Tenderloin with Cherry Salsa, 106–107, *107*
Grilled Fruit Salad, *100,* 101

guacamole
Ancho Chile Asparagus Guacamole, 42, *43*
Sweet Smell of Summer Burgers—Thyme-Infused Teriyaki Burgers with Pineapple Salsa & Guacamole, 70–71, *71*

H

Ham & Pepper Egg Cups, Cheesy, *94,* 95
Haystack Squash Salad—Butternut Brown Sugar Quinoa Bowl, 156–157, *157*
Holiday Breakfast Casserole, 174, *175*

hot dogs
Campfire Coney Dogs, *126,* 127

I

Individual Detroit-Style Pizzas, 178–179, *179*

J

Jalapeño Irish Beer Cheese Soup, *182,* 183
Jalapeño Pineapple Margaritas & Filet Mignon Kabobs, 38, *39*

M

Mama G's Meatloaf & Loaded Potato Bites, 184–185, *185*
Mesquite Lime Chicken Tacos, 186–187, *187*

Michigan
agriculture, 8–10
cherry season, 12–13, 91
outdoor activities, 10
spring, 40
summer, 91

Michigan Cherry Salad with Maple-Cayenne Candied Walnuts and Cherry-Balsamic Vinaigrette, *108,* 109
Michigan Manhattan Cocktails with Ancho Chili Candied Bacon & Bourbon-Soaked Black Cherries Skewer, 34, *35*
Mighty Mac Olive Burger, *68,* 69
Mitten Mac-N-Cheese, *188,* 189
Muffler Meatballs, 130, *131*

mushrooms
Garlicky Mushroom Stuffed Roast Chicken, 158–159, *159*
Spring Morel Risotto with Asparagus & Peas, *60,* 61

O

olives
Mighty Mac Olive Burger, *68,* 69

onions
Apple and Onion Pulled Pork Sandwiches & Nachos, *122, 123*
Defend the Den Burgers Topped with Jalapeño Onion Poppers & Zesty Sauce, 72–73, *73*
Green Bean Casserole Topped with Jalapeño Onion Poppers, 165

P

Pappardelle Pepper-Crusted Beef Ragu, 190, *191*

pasta
Antipasto Salad with Bloody Mary Vinaigrette, *120,* 121
Mitten Mac-N-Cheese, *188,* 189
Pappardelle Pepper-Crusted Beef Ragu, 190, *191*
Soba Noodle Asparagus Chicken Satay, 54, *55*
Summer Veggie Pasta, *112,* 113
Swiss Chicken Pasta Salad, *46, 47*

peaches
Gold Coast Grilled Cheese—Beer-Battered Avocado Grilled Cheese with Chipotle Peach Slaw, 84, *85*
Grilled Fruit Salad, *100,* 101
Peach Bellinis with Mozzarella, Basil & Prosciutto Peach Skewers, *36, 37*
Peach Habanero Mini Burgers, *76,* 77
Shakin' Chipotle Cherry Burgers with Peach Mimosa Salsa & Adobo Avocado Aioli on Pretzel Buns, 74–75, *75*

Pecan Pumpkin Bars with Maple Cream Cheese Frosting, *168,* 169
Pepper-Crusted Pastrami Burgers, 66, *67*
Pepperoni Pizza Zucchini Boats, *104,* 105

peppers
Cheesy Ham & Pepper Egg Cups, *94,* 95

pickles
author's memories, 13–15
Quick Dill Pickles, 110, *111*

Picnic, Charcuterie Board, 124–125, *125*

pie
Apple Crisp Ice Cream Pie Topped with Salted Caramel Frosted Flakes, 166, *167*

pineapple
Silver Sunset Cocktails—Jalapeño Pineapple

INDEX 205

Margaritas & Filet Mignon Kabobs, 38, *39*
Sweet Smell of Summer Burgers—Thyme-Infused Teriyaki Burgers with Pineapple Salsa & Guacamole, 70–71, *71*
Teriyaki Pineapple Chicken with Asparagus in a Pineapple Bowl, 56, *57*

pizza
    Asparagus Crust White Chicken Pizza, 48, *49*
    Individual Detroit-Style Pizzas, 178–179, *179*
    Pepperoni Pizza Zucchini Boats, *104,* 105

pork
    Apple and Onion Pulled Pork Sandwiches & Nachos, 122, *123*
    Grilled Cherry-Chipotle Pork Tenderloin with Cherry Salsa, 106–107, *107*

potatoes
    Canoe Corn Lake Bake, 96, *97*
    Mama G's Meatloaf & Loaded Potato Bites, 184–185, *185*

pot pie
    Chicken Pot Pie Spaghetti Squash, *148,* 149
    Pretzel Crusted Chocolate Cake with Peanut Butter Frosting, 194–195, *195*

pumpkin
    Pecan Pumpkin Bars with Maple Cream Cheese Frosting, *168,* 169

Q
Quick Dill Pickles, 110, *111*
quinoa
    Haystack Squash Salad—Butternut Brown Sugar Quinoa Bowl, 156–157, *157*

R
Rhubarb & Strawberry Pretzel Crumble, 62, *63*
rice
    Spring Morel Risotto with Asparagus & Peas, *60,* 61
Ritzy Rich Bars—Shortbread-Cookie Cheesecake Turtle Bars, 196, *197*

S
salads
    Antipasto Salad with Bloody Mary Vinaigrette, *120,* 121
    Asparagus Spring Salad in Parmesan Cheese Cups, 52, *53*
    Fall Harvest Salad, 152, *153*
    Grilled Fruit Salad, *100,* 101
    Haystack Squash Salad—Butternut Brown Sugar Quinoa Bowl, 156–157, *157*
    Michigan Cherry Salad with Maple-Cayenne Candied Walnuts and Cherry-Balsamic Vinaigrette, *108,* 109
    Strawberry Feta Spinach Salad, 58, *59*
    Swiss Chicken Pasta Salad, *46,* 47
    Watermelon Radish and Romanesco Salmon Salad, *154,* 155
    Wedge Salad, Cowboy Ribeye with Peppercorn Sauce and, 180, *181*
Salami, Mint & Mozzarella Skewers, *26, 27*
Salted Caramel Peanut Butter Toffee Dip, *132,* 133
sandwiches. *See* burgers & sammies
sausage
    Canoe Corn Lake Bake, 96, *97*

Croissant Croque-Madame Burgers, 78–79, *79*
Mama G's Meatloaf & Loaded Potato Bites, 184–185, *185*
Muffler Meatballs, 130, *131*
Pepperoni Pizza Zucchini Boats, *104,* 105
Scotchie Squash Cheesecake Bars, 170–171, *171*
Shakin' Chipotle Cherry Burgers with Peach Mimosa Salsa & Adobo Avocado Aioli on Pretzel Buns, 74–75, *75*
Shortbread-Cookie Cheesecake Turtle Bars, 196, *197*
Silver Sunset Cocktails—Jalapeño Pineapple Margaritas & Filet Mignon Kabobs, 38, *39*

skewers
    Ancho Chili Candied Bacon & Bourbon-Soaked Black Cherries, 34, *35*
    Caramel Apple Cheesecake, 24, *25*
    Chocolate Ganache & Graham Cracker-Toffee S'more, *32,* 33
    Coconut Shrimp, 30–31, *31*
    Filet Mignon Kabobs, 38, *39*
    Mozzarella, Basil & Prosciutto Peach, *36,* 37
    Salami, Mint & Mozzarella, *26, 27*
    Triple Cherry Brownie Bite, *22,* 23

Sloppy Joes, Game Day, *128,* 129
Soba Noodle Asparagus Chicken Satay, 54, *55*

soup
    Jalapeño Irish Beer Cheese Soup, *182,* 183
    Tomato Basil Soup with Cheddar Cheese Crisps, *192,* 193
    Turkey Chili, 140, *141*

Spinach & Artichoke Bacon Bread Bowl, 134–135, *135*
Spring Morel Risotto with Asparagus & Peas, *60,* 61

squash
- Chicken Pot Pie Spaghetti Squash, 148, *149*
- Haystack Squash Salad—Butternut Brown Sugar Quinoa Bowl, 156–157, *157*
- Scotchie Squash Cheesecake Bars, 170–171, *171*
- Summer Veggie Pasta, *112,* 113
- Steelhead Trout in Parchment, 136, *137*

strawberries
- Cherry-Berry Stuffed French Toast Casserole, 98, *99*
- Rhubarb & Strawberry Pretzel Crumble, 62, *63*
- Strawberry Feta Spinach Salad, 58, *59*

Stuffing, Dried Cranberry Sage, 160, *161*

Summer Veggie Pasta, *112,* 113

sweet potatoes
- Apple Cinnamon Loaded Sweet Potatoes, 146, *147*
- Fall Harvest Salad, 152, *153*
- Sweet Smell of Summer Burgers—Thyme-Infused Teriyaki Burgers with Pineapple Salsa & Guacamole, 70–71, *71*

Swiss Chicken Pasta Salad, *46,* 47

T

tacos
- Mesquite Lime Chicken Tacos, 186–187, *187*

Tater Tot Bites, Deluxe, *138,* 139

teriyaki
- Sweet Smell of Summer Burgers—Thyme-Infused Teriyaki Burgers with Pineapple Salsa & Guacamole, 70–71, *71*
- Teriyaki Pineapple Chicken with Asparagus in a Pineapple Bowl, *56,* 57
- Thyme-Infused Teriyaki Burgers with Pineapple Salsa & Guacamole, 70–71, *71*

tomatoes
- Roasted and Toasted Tomato Crostini, 114, *115*
- Tomato Basil Soup with Cheddar Cheese Crisps, *192,* 193

"trailgating"
- Antipasto Salad with Bloody Mary Vinaigrette, *120,* 121
- Apple and Onion Pulled Pork Sandwiches & Nachos, 122, *123*
- Apple Fritter Dip, *142,* 143
- Campfire Coney Dogs, *126,* 127
- Charcuterie Board Picnic, 124–125, *125*
- Deluxe Tater Tot Bites, *138,* 139
- Game Day Sloppy Joes, *128,* 129
- Muffler Meatballs, 130, *131*
- Salted Caramel Peanut Butter Toffee Dip, *132,* 133
- Spinach & Artichoke Bacon Bread Bowl, 134–135, *135*
- Steelhead Trout in Parchment, 136, *137*
- Turkey Chili, 140, *141*

Triple Cherry Brownies, *116,* 117

turkey
- Cheesy Enchiladas, *176,* 177
- Turkey Chili, 140, *141*

V

vegetables. *See also* specific vegetables
- Canoe Corn Lake Bake, 96, *97*
- Fall Harvest Salad, 152, *153*
- Summer Veggie Pasta, *112,* 113

W

Watermelon Radish and Romanesco Salmon Salad, *154,* 155

Z

zucchini
- Pepperoni Pizza Zucchini Boats, *104,* 105
- Summer Veggie Pasta, *112,* 113